HAUNTED HOTELS IN AMERICA

Robin Mead

THOMAS NELSON
Since 1798

Haunted Hotels in America

© 1995, 2022 Robin Mead

Originally published as *Haunted Hotels: A Guide to American and Canadian Inns and Their Ghosts*

All rights reserved. No portion of this book may be reproduced, stored in a retrieval system, or transmitted in any form or by any means—electronic, mechanical, photocopy, recording, scanning, or other—except for brief quotations in critical reviews or articles, without the prior written permission of the publisher.

Published in Nashville, Tennessee, by Thomas Nelson. Thomas Nelson is a registered trademark of HarperCollins Christian Publishing, Inc.

Additional content written and revised by Rachel McMillan

Thomas Nelson titles may be purchased in bulk for educational, business, fundraising, or sales promotional use. For information, please email SpecialMarkets@ThomasNelson.com.

Any internet addresses, phone numbers, or company or product information printed in this book are offered as a resource and are not intended in any way to be or to imply an endorsement by Thomas Nelson, nor does Thomas Nelson vouch for the existence, content, or services of these sites, phone numbers, companies, or products beyond the life of this book.

ISBN 978-0-7852-9329-3 (audio)
ISBN 978-0-7852-9328-6 (ebook)
ISBN 978-0-7852-9327-9 (TP)

Library of Congress Cataloging-in-Publication Data On File

Printed in the United States of America
22 23 24 25 26 LSC 6 5 4 3 2 1

ACKNOWLEDGMENTS

This book could not have been written without the assistance of and information provided by the Travel Industry Association of America and many state tourist boards (especially those of California, Maine, Maryland, and Wyoming). Special thanks for advice and assistance are also due to the National Trust for Historic Preservation; Ritz-Carlton Hotels; and Best Western.

The author also thanks the following individuals for their help and ideas, much of it provided above and beyond the call of duty: Rachel McMillan, Valerie Field, Mary Kay Cline, Anita Cotter, Hugh DeStamper, Charlotte Fenn, Polly Larner, Sarah Graham Mann, Anne North, Fred Slater, and Martha Steger.

INTRODUCTION

Do you believe in ghosts? I have asked that question hundreds of times during my lectures and the results are always the same. People are almost equally divided between believers and those who think ghost stories are just that, stories.

This can create a problem for the historic hotels and inns that are believed to have one or more nonpaying residents in the form of a ghost. Do you keep quiet about it to avoid frightening nervous guests? Or do you make a feature of your phantom and tell everyone that there is great fun to be had by taking a family vacation in a haunted hotel?

For hotel owners who can't quite make up their minds, it is worth remembering that the first question many guests ask when checking into a historic property is "Do you have a ghost?" It is also a fact that many alleged "haunted" hotels and inns are booked for months, and even years, in advance.

In *Haunted Hotels in America* you will find a selection of places to stay that cheerfully admit to having an intangible guest or two. The stories are extraordinarily varied. Some are sad. Some are puzzling. A few are even funny. The spirit world is not without its sense of humor.

Inside you'll read about ghosts who've established quite frightening reputations that span over a century. You'll also be introduced to chilling hauntings that have inspired popular documentaries and

Hollywood films. If you decide to embark on your own haunting adventure, there's a checklist of all the hotels and inns featured in *Haunted Hotels in America*.

Happy Ghost Hunting,

Robin Mead

CONTENTS

CONTENTS

MALAGA INN

Mobile, Alabama

The Malaga Inn captures the glory of the antebellum period, even though it was built after the beginning of the War between the States in 1862. Originally constructed as two neighboring houses for brothers-in-law Isaac Goldsmith and William Frohlichstein, the Italianate-style homes were a gorgeous boutique extension to keep the men and their wives, close sisters together. During the time of construction, the war was still going well for the South and the brothers-in-law's business partnership of the Brisk and Jacobson Store in downtown Mobile was booming. Guests intrigued by the family history of the inn will find that the store's four-story cast-iron facade is as beautiful as it is unique and worth a visit. There are three basic room types for accommodation all outfitted with period replica furniture. Breakfast is served daily and Wi-Fi is free. The courtyard with its garden and romantic atmosphere is a popular place to retreat all times of year. The central location gives guests easy access by car or foot to many of Mobile's nearby sites.

The Malaga Inn serves as a popular destination during Mardi Gras with colorful flags draped over the balconies and revelers overtaking the courtyards. But just as the period of prosperity for Goldsmith and Frohlichstein waned during the war and its Reconstruction period, so the Malaga fell out of the family. That doesn't mean, however, that their influence is not felt around the premises.

 THE GHOST of the Malaga Inn is believed to be one of the two sisters who prefers to inhabit Room 007, dressed in white and pacing the balcony. Guests have reported chandeliers swinging of their own accord and furniture moving on its own. A feature on the Malaga on Amazon Prime finds medium Ericka Boussarhane visiting the hotel with truly chilling results and recorded paranormal activity. Some of the hauntings may well begin in a tunnel connecting the two once-divided houses. In contrast to the grand facade of the Malaga, this crude subterranean brick underpass is theorized as a hidden escape for Confederate soldiers. Whatever presences exist above and below ground, the Malaga is a picture-perfect homage to the glory of the South. The ghost in 007 may just be attempting to join in the Mardi Gras festivities—like Scarlett O'Hara in her flouncy gown—clinging to a glorious antebellum period that will never return.

Malaga Inn

Address: 359 Church St., Mobile, AL 36602
Website: www.malagainn.com

Alaska

THE HISTORIC ANCHORAGE HOTEL

Anchorage, Alaska

Established in 1916 and now listed on the National Registry of Historic Places, the uniquely fascinating Anchorage Hotel is near the Alaska Zoo, the Anchorage Museum (with plenty of gold-rush-era history), and Denali National Park. Airy and spacious, the hotel hosts a wood-paneled bar that seems like a snapshot of its earliest years complete with stuffed elk head and moose antlers. Guests can book one of twenty-six rooms and expect free parking, easy access to many of Anchorage's sites, and a complimentary breakfast buffet. The friendly front desk staff will be happy to help guests navigate the numerous festivals and activities that lure locals and visitors alike and to select the best and most family appropriate of the many day excursion and museum offerings.

THE GHOST of the Historic Anchorage Hotel is "Black Jack" Sturgus: Anchorage's first police chief, who was shot in the back with his own gun. In the *East Bay Times*, general manager Terri Russell recalls one instance when a painting flew across the room "so hard it shattered the whole frame . . . How do you explain that?"

The explanation seems to be Sturgus.

He is also the supposed reason for feet being poked in the middle of the night, a man's reflection in the mirror, and wineglasses clinking in a phantom "cheers." The hotel is such a hotbed of paranormal activity that a thick log of guests' voluntarily recorded encounters would make for hours-long reading.

The hotel is proud of its ghostly rumors, though. Their website proudly displays NBC coverage from the Today Show. "Curtains rumbling, shower curtains swaying, pictures flying . . . it's all par for the course."

Yet Sturgus's death has never been solved, giving a treat to amateur detectives and ghost hunters alike. When the mystery of Sturgus's killer is finally solved, the Anchorage may finally be able to rest in peace.

The Historic Anchorage Hotel

Address: 330 E St., Anchorage, AK 99501
Website: www.historicanchoragehotel.com

COPPER QUEEN HOTEL

Bisbee, Arizona

A beautiful old property, "the Queen" was built by the Copper Queen Mining Company in the very early part of the twentieth century when Bisbee, high in the hills and close to the Mexican border, was the world's largest mining town. The Queen still dominates the attractive little town and is being lovingly restored to its original grandeur.

There are forty-five comfortable guest rooms, all with every modern convenience. The public rooms are particularly atmospheric: they include two lobbies, the traditionally styled Copper Queen Saloon, an excellent dining room, and a patio where meals and drinks are available. The hotel has its own swimming pool.

The townspeople still visit the Copper Queen for a cocktail or a few beers in the evening, just as they've always done. And although men such as "Black Jack" Pershing and the young Teddy Roosevelt, who once frequented the hotel, are long gone, the town's new settlers—artists, writers, and filmmakers—are just as interesting to meet and talk with.

Bisbee's copper mines can still be visited. Outfitted with yellow slickers and miners' lamps, groups descend deep into the shafts of the abandoned Copper Queen Mine before catching the cramped mining train back to the surface. Tours are also available to the Lavender Pit Mine, one of the world's largest open pit mines.

Aboveground, the clear skies and accommodating climate of this mile-high town make for great tennis, swimming, hiking, golf, and sightseeing. Rock collectors go in search of mineral specimens, which include the famous "Bisbee Blue Turquoise." Souvenir shopping is excellent. Historic Tombstone, site of the famous shoot-out at the O.K. Corral, is just a twenty-minute drive away.

 THERE ARE BELIEVED TO BE THREE RESIDENT GHOSTS AT Copper Queen, one who seems to spend most of her time on the third floor. But strange happenings are a regular occurrence throughout the beautiful old building. So much so, in fact, that staff keep a huge ledger on the reception desk where both employees and guests are asked to record any odd happenings. It makes strange reading.

"Weird things have happened to people who work here," former general manager Peter Pieth once said. One night porter, for example, watched in amazement as the main doors in the entrance hall swung open and a light appeared to emerge from one of the big mirrors in the lobby, move around, then float up the grand staircase and finally disappear.

Another night auditor experienced strange nocturnal phenomena. She theorized: "Whatever or whoever it is, it likes young guys." That would seem to be borne out by the experience of a good-looking chief engineer at the hotel, who stepped into the empty elevator and was alarmed to find an invisible presence breathing heavily beside him. Or the easy-on-the-eyes bodyguard, looking after a movie star staying at the Copper Queen, who left his room in terror and refused to return after repeatedly hearing a husky voice murmuring "Hello" in his ear.

The most haunted rooms are thought to be Room 305 and Room 315, although two women guests who stayed in Room 312 reported that a hat belonging to neither of them kept flying around the room—an occurrence reported elsewhere in the hotel. Other slightly less inexplicable oddities include alarm clocks with minds of their own, and odd buzzing noises.

"We don't know who the lady is," Peter Pieth once said. "But we do know she likes men. Perhaps someone was once murdered on the third floor. In a mining town like this, lots of things have happened since 1902."

More recently, the Copper Queen has been the subject of paranormal investigation shows such as *Ghost Hunters* and *Ghost Adventurers*. Both believe the ghost is a young woman named Julia Lowell. Lowell, a prostitute who fell in unrequited love with a client and took her own life upon his rejection, corroborates the belief that the ghost prefers flirting with members of the opposite sex, dancing provocatively, and even whispering in their ears or tickling their feet. Julia Lowell may be the only ghost to have an eponymous room, but a gentleman who descends the staircases with a top hat and cape, in a fog of cigar smoke, also makes an appearance. Most chillingly, the most haunting figure is the third ghost: a little boy who drowned in the nearby San Pedro River. While never seen, his giggle can be heard along with his light footsteps in the hallway.

Copper Queen Hotel

Address: 11 Howell Ave., Bisbee, Arizona 85603
Website: www.copperqueen.com/haunted-hotels-arizona

HOTEL VENDOME

Prescott, Arizona

A charming and pleasantly restored 1917 lodging house, the Hotel Vendome has twenty-five newly designed bedrooms within its original walls. Each room has either a queen-size bed or twin beds, with its own bathroom, Wi-Fi, and cable. There are also two-room suites available.

The rooms have all been individually decorated to make the most of the available space and light. Original wide woodworking has been retained and is complemented by oak furnishings, period wallpapers, country-print fabrics, and brass ceiling fans.

The comfortable lobby has a cozy little bar in one corner, hand-fashioned in cherry by local craftsmen. It features a custom-made wine boutique, serving both domestic and imported wines and beers. In all, this is a simple property, but with a comfortable and relaxed atmosphere.

The mile-high town of Prescott is a comfortable drive from Flagstaff, Phoenix, or Tucson, and close to the beauty of Sedona and the mystery of Jerome. The town is noted for its ideal climate, its twenty thousand easy-living and friendly residents, and its enthusiasm for the great outdoors. And what an outdoors! Prescott is surrounded by the beautiful Bradshaw Mountains and the ponderosa pines of Groom Creek.

Summers are mild, autumns crisp, and the sunsets spectacular in these parts. Local attractions include the holiday lighting of Prescott's Courthouse Plaza at Christmas, the excitement of Frontier Days on the Fourth of July, and the treasures in the historic Sharlot Hall Museum.

THE GHOST at the Hotel Vendome is Abby, who died in 1925 but still lives in Room 16. And Abby is not alone. She is accompanied by her cat, Noble.

Rama Patel, one-time owner of the hotel, even referred to Room 16 as "Abby's Room." She explained that one-time owner Abby lost the hotel when she didn't pay her taxes. The new owner, however, let her stay at the property, which she thought of as home. When Abby fell sick, she sent her husband out for some medicine but for reasons unknown he didn't return. Left alone, sick, and starving, Abby passed away in the room. So, it appears, did Noble.

Since then, guests staying in Room 16 have reported a variety of unexplained incidents. The TV set has turned on and off by itself, and amateur ghost hunters reported "contacting" Abby in the room. Years ago, as the stories spread, Mary Woodhouse, a reporter for the local newspaper, the *Daily Courier*, and photographer Marcy Rogers spent a night in the haunted room.

"I believe Abby paid me a visit," Woodhouse said afterward. The radiators kept turning off during the night, leaving the room feeling cold, and she was awakened by the sound of a cat meowing even though she couldn't find a trace of the animal.

Despite such incidents, Abby and Noble are likely to remain in Prescott for a long time to come.

"Abby is part of the Hotel Vendome," says Rama Patel. "We don't want her to leave."

Hotel Vendome

Address: 230 S. Cortez St., Prescott, AZ 86301

Website: www.vendomehotel.com

CRESCENT HOTEL AND SPA
Eureka Springs, Arkansas

Called "the Grand Lady of the Ozarks," the Crescent Hotel's beauty is rivaled by its surrounding mountains. Since its opening in 1886, guests have been lured by its perch amid natural beauty and its proximity to Eureka's restorative hot springs. A longtime resort for the rich and famous, its original architecture, designed by Isaac Taylor, was carefully planned so that guests were afforded a majestic view of the valley below. Irish stonemasons used limestone in its construction and the Richardsonian Romanesque–revival structure houses some of the most fascinating and haunted lore in American hotel history.

The Crescent has lived as many lives as the tabby cat Morris who took up residence in the hotel in 1973 and is one in a long line of felines who have populated the grand hotel since its early years. Today, it features seventy-two rooms and four luxury cottages with a hot tub and swimming pool available for guest enjoyment and over fifteen acres of manicured gardens to explore. The New Moon Spa and Salon on-site is a modern incarnation of the hotel's rich history as a restorative and relaxing part of the state. There are several dining options including breakfast and dinner at the Crystal Dining Room and Sky Bar Gourmet Pizza. The Top of the Crest bar offers frozen drinks and snacks and a fantastic view while the Frisco BBQ Bus provides guests with an on-site food truck experience for a quick dinner or snack.

THE GHOSTS of the Crescent Hotel are the patients of charlatan quack doctor Norman Baker who operated a hospital on the grounds entitled "Baker's Cancer Curing Hospital." Suddenly the restorative properties of Eureka's nearby springs were given a run for the money by the philandering Baker who preyed on the then-proprietor's concern for his wife's failing health. Medical Maverick Baker posited a cure via his magical elixir of watermelon seed, brown corn silk, alcohol, and carbolic acid. Unsurprisingly, the cure was found more than lacking and, sadly, many of the good "doctor's" patients perished at such an alarming rate that a morgue was constructed in the basement.

Years after Baker's swindling, he followed his life of crime to Florida while the Crescent made long strides toward restoring its grandeur beyond its years of disarray and its sad makeshift "hospital." But the victims of Baker's scheme seemed to be experiencing anything but a restful peace.

Baker's carnivalesque cancer cures have left the Crescent with not one supposed specter but many, representing the many duped by the doctor and enacting their revenge. Guests have smelled cherry tobacco rumored to have been a favorite of a doctor in residence long before Baker while others have experienced the trickery of a bookish ghost who is known for throwing library books at unsuspecting guests.

Several years ago, the SyFy Channel hired mediums to "read" the building for paranormal phenomena and interviewed one of the ghostly tour guides. The guide had recorded several guests fainting and passing out. The hotel's blog goes into detail about the morbid occurrences about the position of every incident: the area near a portal directly above the old morgue where Baker's cancer patients perished.

Ghost tours are available for guests, though may not be needed, for if firsthand accounts are true, you need not go in pursuit of the Crescent's ghosts—they'll already be in pursuit of you.

Crescent Hotel and Spa

Address: 75 Prospect Ave., Eureka Springs, AR 72632

Website: www.crescent-hotel.com

THE CARTER HOUSE
Eureka, California

The Carter House is a beautifully furnished bed-and-breakfast in a stylish reproduction Victorian mansion in this northern California seaport.

Mark and Christie Carter have furnished it in elegant style with period pieces culled from stock when, in the late 1980s, they lived in the newly built house and ran an antiques business from home. Now they reside in nearby Eureka while tending to their guests.

The rooms here are very spacious, bold in decor, and contain some wonderful early Victorian oak and walnut bedsteads and armoires. All the rooms have a private bath with pet-friendly rooms available on request.

The entrance floor has a comfortable lounge-library with panoramic views over the harbor. Modern works of art hang throughout, and it is a tribute to the Carter family's taste that the overall effect is that of an intimate art gallery. Award-winning restaurant 301 is where guests can enjoy fine dining as well as sample a selection of Envy wines produced in nearby Napa Valley and partnering with the

Carter House. For those who prefer whiskey, the Old Carter Whiskey Company offers tastings and samples at the bar.

THE GHOST at the Carter House is not exactly an apparition; it's a set of extraordinary and somewhat chilling coincidences.

Innkeeper Mark Carter, already busy with the Hotel Carter, yearned to fill a vacant lot kitty-corner from it with a Victorian mansion where he could live with his family. He could visualize exactly the kind of house that would suit the corner plot. But where could he find an architect or a set of plans to re-create the distinctive Victorian-Gothic style he envisioned? Diligent inquiries over a prolonged period in the 1980s produced nothing that seemed quite right.

Eventually, a friend in San Francisco came across a folio of old architects' drawings: pages and pages of plans for mansions of all shapes and sizes, dating from the 1870s. Still, when Carter browsed through it, nothing seemed to fit his ideal.

Then, toward the end of the volume, there appeared a plan of a house drawn up by the Newsom brothers and built in 1884 for the Murphy family on Bush and Jones in San Francisco. Although the house is now demolished, it was exactly how Carter had imagined his dream house for the lot in Eureka, right down to the last scalloped shingle and fretwork dado.

Thus was born the Carter House in Eureka, a meticulous reincarnation of the Murphy House completed in 1989.

So what's spooky about that? Despite Mark Carter's long quest for exactly the right design for his vacant plot, the Newsom plans could easily have escaped his notice.

But Eureka just happens to have two other beautiful Newsom

houses, both within a block of where the Carter House now stands. There is the hugely magnificent, masculine, and slightly reptilian Carson Mansion (now the exclusive Ingomar Club) and, opposite it, the stunning Carson House—more delicate, pastel toned, and known as "the Pink Lady."

Just coincidence? Suffice to say, the Carter House is the house that "asked" to be built.

The Carter House
Address: 1033 3rd St., Eureka, CA 95501
Website: www.carterhouse.com

THE CLIFT ROYAL SONESTA
San Francisco, California

Opened in 1915, the seventeen-story Clift Royal Sonesta Hotel remains one of the top hotels in San Francisco. It stands in the heart of the city, very close to Union Square, and sets the standard for luxury accommodations and attentive personalized service.

The 329 beautifully appointed guest rooms and suites are spacious, with high ceilings, restored moldings and woodwork, fine Georgian reproductions, and marble bathrooms. Each room is climate-controlled with windows opening to the crisp San Francisco air.

Frederick's eatery and café boasts creative food and drink and Eat Local SF ensures guests are indulging in locally sourced dishes. For upscale dining, the magnificent art deco Redwood Room cocktail lounge and piano bar is a San Francisco landmark and favorite meeting place in its own right. It was built from a single two-thousand-year-old redwood tree from the forests of northern California and has been restored to its original luster.

While the hotel's recent renovation boasts modern touches, the hotel's iconic legacy is preserved with traditional touches that recall the elegance of its past including the restored and rehung original artwork of noted Viennese painter Gustav Klimt.

Superbly situated within a very short walk of the city center, the famed Geary Street theaters, and plenty of fine boutiques and upscale department stores. Chinatown and the financial district are easily accessible.

 THE GHOST is Robert Odell, a larger-than-life character who once owned the property. He haunts the rooftop: a once self-contained seven-hundred-square-foot apartment he used as a permanent residence.

The Clift Royal takes its name from Frederick Clift, a lawyer whose father owned land at the corner of Geary and Taylor Streets at the time of the San Francisco earthquake on April 18, 1906. Soon after the quake, and the fire that followed, Frederick Clift inherited his father's land. At a time when the city was rebuilding itself, he resolved to erect a regally styled and earthquake-proof hotel on the city's center site.

Clift gave the job of designing his dream property to George Applegarth, an ambitious young architect. Applegarth—pioneering the use of steel-reinforced concrete—planned a property destined to profoundly affect much of San Francisco's architecture and the way the city looks today. The original twelve-story hotel opened in 1915, with Clift taking up residence in the rooftop stone bungalow that later became known as the fashionable Spanish Suite.

Clift died in 1936, but before his death, various financial deals passed the property to a thirty-six-year-old Iowan venture capitalist, Robert Odell. Odell promptly ordered the closure and complete renovation of the Clift. When the hotel reopened in 1936, the magnificent Redwood Room was unveiled, as one of the prime examples of art deco in the entire Bay Area.

Odell moved into the Spanish Suite with his wife, Helen. He was an imposing man, six foot six in stature and with piercing eyes. Odell was extremely strong and many of his employees were terrified of him, especially when he had been drinking. Staff would sound an alarm to warn one another when he returned from a night on the town. His hobby was breaking horses, but more than that, he was a bon vivant. He and Helen and their new-look hotel were a sensation. The hotel restaurant, over which Odell kept close control, became one of the most fashionable in the city. The guest list read like an international who's who.

Success continued for years. Odell and his managers pioneered many of what are now accepted practices among top hoteliers. The Odell era did not end until June 1973, and Odell ended it by his own hand. He committed suicide in the Spanish Suite.

The stories began at once. Employees claimed the suite was haunted and refused to enter it.

Staff and guest alike watched in astonishment as the doors finally slammed themselves shut with such force that the wood cracked.

Now the famous rooftop hosts ten hives and ten thousand honeybees in line with the hotel's environmentally conscious initiatives. Thus, the Spanish Suite has been sacrificed to the modern reincarnation of the building. Searching Trip Advisor and Travelocity comments for haunted experiences leads to some dead-end searches of *comment deleted*: perhaps in an attempt to sweep the morbid past under the proverbial carpet. But some guests just refuse to leave no matter how extensive a remodel.

The Clift Royal Sonesta
Address: 495 Geary St., San Francisco, CA 94102
Website: www.sonesta.com/us/california/san-francisco
/clift-royal-sonesta-hotel

HOTEL DEL CORONADO
Coronado, California

Coronado Island, situated in San Diego Bay and accessible by a two-mile long bridge, is famous for two things: its huge U.S. Navy base and the vast, red-roofed Hotel del Coronado. Looking like "an oversized pigeon loft," in the words of one writer, "the Del" is said to have been the inspiration for the Emerald City in *The Wizard of Oz* and the setting for the classic Marilyn Monroe film *Some Like It Hot*—although in the latter case the scriptwriters moved it to Florida.

The hotel also has an odd place in history. It is believed to be where Edward, Prince of Wales, first met Mrs. Wallis Simpson, then a U.S. Navy officer's wife, in the ballroom in 1920. Sixteen years later the Prince of Wales was to rock the British throne by abdicating to marry the by-then-divorced Mrs. Simpson.

Opened in 1888, the Del has grown into the largest resort property on the Pacific coast. The hotel claims to have hosted more celebrities than any other hotel in the United States. It is a national historic landmark and is listed in the National Register of Historic Places.

As has always been the case, today's guests want for nothing. Every room in the main Victorian building has been painstakingly restored and is one of a kind in its decor. Modern rooms, like those in the Ocean Tower, blend the accoutrements of the past with all modern amenities, including air conditioning. Rooms offer magnificent views of the Pacific Ocean, the cityscape of San Diego Bay, the yachts of Glorietta Harbor, and flower-filled courtyards containing such rarities as one of America's only dragon trees (a native of the Canary Islands).

The facilities seem endless. There are eight restaurants and lounges, including two top dinner venues: the Ocean Terrace with its panoramic Pacific views, and the opulent Crown Room with its gilt-edged china and tuxedo-clad waiters. There are heated pools, a spa, a series of waterfront tennis courts, and Coronado's nearby eighteen-hole bayside golf course. Seaborne activities available at the Del's boathouse include sailing, fishing, and whale-watching excursions.

 THE GHOST at the Hotel del Coronado is Kate Morgan, who either committed suicide at the hotel or was murdered there by her husband on November 29, 1892. In either case, she never checked out. Kate's room, now Room 3312, is said to be haunted, as is a former maid's room, Room 3502. Kate also fiddles with the phones and tampers with the television—and before you laugh that off, it has to be said this is one of the best-documented and most famous of America's hotel ghost stories.

Kate, a beautiful brunette wearing black nineteenth-century

clothes, has often been seen gliding down the hotel's corridors or standing by the windows as if waiting for someone. Perhaps that someone is her husband, the card shark Tom Morgan. When they were traveling through Los Angeles by train in November 1892, Kate told her husband she was pregnant. The couple quarreled and Tom disembarked, but he did promise to meet Kate in San Diego for Thanksgiving.

Kate, twenty-seven, checked into the Hotel del Coronado on Thanksgiving Day, November 24. For some reason, she gave her name as Lottie A. Bernard of Detroit. Her husband did not arrive to join her, and after a couple of days Kate complained of pains. She then took a ferry to San Diego, bought herself a .44-caliber gun, and left a message for Tom at another hotel, the Hotel Brewster, before returning to the Coronado. No one knows what happened that night, but the next day Kate was found dead on the steps leading from the hotel's north entrance to a sand walk. She had been shot in the head and a single bullet was missing from the gun in her hand. Suicide? Perhaps. But the bullet that killed Kate Morgan was a .38-caliber or .40-caliber, from a different gun.

More than one hundred years later, the mystery still has not been solved. In his book *The Legend of Kate Morgan: The Search for the Ghost of the Hotel del Coronado*, attorney Alan M. May concluded that Kate was murdered by her returning husband. A former army buddy of May's, Gerry Rush, has gone even further. He contends Tom Morgan also killed the maid (Room 3502) who looked after Kate—she disappeared the day after Kate's funeral.

One weakness of these theories is that Tom Morgan was never seen at the Hotel del Coronado. Nonetheless, the reports of strange happenings in Rooms 3312 and 3502 continue unabated. Local historian Richard Carico slept in one of the haunted rooms in 1988 and heard "faint murmurings." In 1990, Rush claimed, he heard a woman crying in the corridor. When he asked her what was the matter, the woman replied, "I was murdered. It is not only Kate Morgan in the ground. It is I, the housekeeper." Parapsychologist Christopher Chacon can find nothing out of the ordinary in Kate's room, Room 3312, but says of Room 3502: "It's a classic haunting." One-time hotel public relations director Nancy Weisinger was in Room 3502 when *Ghostbusters* star Dan Aykroyd's brother Tom, who really is a ghostbuster, set up some scientific equipment in the room.

"I heard the ashtray flip over," she recalls, "and a glass shattered in the bathroom. It didn't just break; it was as if someone threw it."

Less dramatically, countless guests have reported strange faults on the telephones and inexplicable images appearing on their TV sets. May thought he saw Kate Morgan's face on his TV screen, but as he also decided that she was his great-great-grandmother, perhaps his evidence can be discounted.

In some ways, the stories of Kate Morgan and the ghost of the Del have suffered from being told too often. But one impressive witness was travel agent Jeanie Hawkins, a very down-to-earth businesswoman. When I told her that I was writing this book, she said, "I know a hotel in California that you must include. It is called the Hotel del Coronado. Now that really is haunted."

She arrived there late one evening on a business trip and went straight to bed in the old part of the hotel without hearing any of the Kate Morgan stories. She remembers: "I couldn't sleep. There was a presence in my room. I didn't know it was haunted when I arrived, but there is certainly something there. I have stayed in hotels all over the world, and I've never come across anything like it before."

Was it sad Kate who disturbed Hawkins's slumbers? Or her disappearing maid? Or simply jet lag? Perhaps we will never know.

Hotel del Coronado
Address: 1500 Orange Ave., Coronado, CA 92118
Website: www.hoteldel.com

ABIGAIL'S ELEGANT VICTORIAN MANSION

Eureka, California

Just when you think California's booming bed-and-breakfast industry can't spring any more surprises, you discover this place: an elegant Victorian mansion that—just to make sure there is no confusion—calls itself Abigail's Elegant Victorian Mansion.

Just a few blocks from Eureka's historic Old Town, and set in a quiet, genteel residential neighborhood, the Elegant Victorian Mansion is a restored architectural masterpiece. Designated a national historical landmark, the mansion offers guests a comfortable and price-efficient experience as the current owners have replaced the traditional B-and-B breakfast experience with vastly reduced rates and complimentary all-day tea and coffee. Bathrobes and fluffy towels are provided for guests either in the Governor's Room (which hosts its own en suite bathroom) and the Langtry Rooms (which share a large bathroom).

This is a lovely place.

Eureka, a former logging town with a new lease on life, has many splendid houses. An Elegant Victorian Mansion is one living up to its name. And guests can enjoy a bit of the spirit of long ago with the unique opportunity of a ride in an authentic 1928 Model T Ford!

THE GHOST at the Elegant Victorian Mansion is that of an unknown and unseen woman with a taste for traditional jazz.

Previous owners recall a guest professing to be a medium who explained the rear parlor had a spirit in it. She offered to release the "trapped" spirit, but they declined.

Thereafter, guests reported strange happenings to the then-owners the Vieyras. There was the woman guest in the Van Gogh Room, for example, who knocked on the Vieyras' bedroom door one night early in 1995 to complain that "a ghost had opened her door." Vieyra advised her to lock it, but the door again opened. He then advised her to bolt it, but the door again opened. The woman was considerably shaken—it's worth adding that by profession she was a reputable forensic scientist. Furthermore, I inspected the door less than two months after the incident, and it is impossible to see how it can be opened by anyone or anything once bolted.

But an even more mysterious incident happened the previous year when the Vieyras were away at an innkeepers' convention and left a woman friend house-sitting.

"When we got back, she told us she had been awakened by music coming from downstairs," Doug says. "It went on for some time, then stopped and started again."

The Elegant Victorian Mansion is equipped with an electronic alarm system. The house sitter knew it was impossible for anyone to have broken into the property without her knowing. So, assuming she had left a radio or TV set on, she got out of bed and went downstairs with a flashlight to see what was happening.

She found an old hand-cranked horn phonograph playing by itself. "That just can't happen," Vieyra says. "But it did."

He pointed out the phonograph and explained how it had to be wound between each playing. The house sitter had heard it play twice, so it must have been wound twice. Moreover, whoever—or whatever—played the machine had carefully chosen the pride of Vieyra's record collection: a 1928 recording of the Duke Ellington band playing "St. Louis Blues" with, says Vieyra, "Crosby crooning, Armstrong on trumpet, and Benny Goodman on the clarinet." The alarmed house sitter spent the rest of the night cowering on the stairs.

Oddly, after all this, the Vieyras remain skeptics. As her husband told the phonograph story, Lily Vieyra commented, "I would love that to happen to me. Then I could become a believer."

Strange happenings continue. Doors in the house seem to open of their own accord, then slam shut again. Things disappear. "Big things, like fruit bowls," Lily Vieyra says. "We say that the house is playing with us again." Her husband adds, "I expect there is a logical explanation, but I haven't worked it out yet."

Decades later, it will be up to current guests to decide whether the Vieyra's missed an opportunity. Or whether Abigail's Elegant mansion is destined to be haunted forevermore.

Abigail's Elegant Victorian Mansion

Address: 1406 C St., Eureka, CA 95501
Website: www.eureka-california.com

GINGERBREAD MANSION INN

Ferndale, California

This is an extraordinary bed-and-breakfast in an extraordinary village. Both seem to have been left behind in a time warp. Visitors take a step back into the elegant Victorian age one hundred years ago.

The Gingerbread Mansion itself is one of the most photographed buildings in northern California. Built in 1898 as a doctor's residence, it later became a hospital. Exquisitely decorated with "gingerbread" trim, the beautiful Queen Anne Eastlake Victorian property was lovingly restored by Ken Torbert to create one of the most exquisite bed-and-breakfasts in America in Humboldt County, the heart of redwood country.

There are eleven guest bedrooms in this state historic landmark, including four spectacular suites. They are all beautifully furnished, all have private bathrooms with showers, and they come filled with extras like toweling robes and the wherewithal for bubble baths.

Ferndale itself is a Victorian treasure house of historic homes, churches, and other buildings. Even the shops seem stuck in another age, fun to explore. The town does put on lively theatrical performances. But voyages of exploration on foot are the principal pastime, including to opulent Victorian homes similar to the Gingerbread Mansion, known locally as "Butterfat Palaces," and ornate stone buildings such as the Masonic Hall. The house and the picturesque town have been deemed "a photographer's paradise." Given the colorful nature of these Victorian abodes, you might not even need an Instagram filter! History is all around you. At the Gingerbread Mansion you will be staying in the best-looking bit of it.

 TWO OF THE GHOSTS at the Gingerbread Mansion Inn are presumed to be a couple of mischievous Victorian children, although nobody is quite sure who exactly they were, when they lived there, or what they are doing. The other guests stem from the time when the house functioned as a hospital.

The building's perished patients are rumored to still be in residence. A picture that Torbert hung in the front parlor mysteriously moved itself into the lounge.

Guests walking up the main staircase have slipped on the slightly short thirteenth stair and claimed they were pushed. And one guest, Christopher Earls, spending the night of his twentieth birthday in a suite, awoke "too frightened to turn over" because he "thought there was something there."

Torbert's wife, Sandie, told of two women guests who arrived from San Francisco saying they had come to the Gingerbread Mansion because their friends had "talked about the children." The guests who record their own experience in the guest book have also mentioned somber Victorian faces and odd happenings. A recent Trip Advisor review loved the ambience and atmosphere of the nineteenth-century architecture as well as the hospitality—at least the living human hospitality. The review starts "There's something off." As the guest felt a lingering, observing presence and even a dark shadow leaning above the railing watching them. But for guests who don't mind pulling up a figurative chair and welcoming the other presences who have yet to move out from the Queen Anne mansion, it is hard to imagine a more peaceful and comfortable inn. Relax, and the mind plays tricks. And there can be few more relaxing places than the Gingerbread Mansion Inn.

Gingerbread Mansion Inn
Address: 400 Berding St., Ferndale, CA 95536
Website: www.facebook.com/GingerbreadMansionInn

HORTON GRAND HOTEL
San Diego, California

The Horton Grand Hotel used to be the Grand Horton. It also used to be the Brooklyn. Both of these hotels, built in 1886, were part of a boom in San Diego's history. Modern-day developer Dan Pearson got the idea of giving both old properties a new lease on life by pulling them down and using the parts to create a new hotel. The result is the Horton Grand, an ultramodern property opened in 1986 with many original Victorian features.

The hotel, at the heart of the historic Gaslamp Quarter, is an impressive, four-story building consisting of two "wings" connected at street level by a modern glass atrium that encloses the lobby. The two wings differ. The one on the right as you face the hotel is straightforward Victorian; the one on the left is slightly more elegant with a touch of gingerbread styling. The external brickwork, bay windows, door frames,

and internal main stairway all date from 1886. A popular place for conferences and meetings, the hotel also honors a century-old tradition of
hosting weddings in its courtyard. For fine dining, Salt and Whiskey
is a bar and restaurant keeping in the hotel's motif of a Victorian and
modern blend. Guests can enjoy dinner after a day of sightseeing or
unwind with a selection from their extensive cocktail menu.

Seasonal events—such as leave-the-kids pumpkin carving—are
an additional draw to this trendy spot.

For sightseeing trips around San Diego, horse-drawn carriages
and the Old Town trolleys are right outside the main entrance. The
Horton Plaza shopping center and the convention center are two
blocks away.

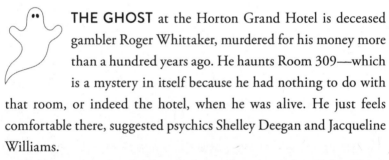

THE GHOST at the Horton Grand Hotel is deceased
gambler Roger Whittaker, murdered for his money more
than a hundred years ago. He haunts Room 309—which
is a mystery in itself because he had nothing to do with
that room, or indeed the hotel, when he was alive. He just feels
comfortable there, suggested psychics Shelley Deegan and Jacqueline
Williams.

Almost immediately after the bits and pieces of the old San Diego
hotels were used to construct the Horton Grand Hotel, staff started
to complain that "strange things were going on" in Room 309. The
lights went on and off of their own accord; a bed shook; pictures were
moved around when the room was empty.

"What really got me one day was when a closet door flew open,"
former housemaid Martha Mayes says. "I never saw a ghost, but some
people say they did."

Those people include a woman guest who walked down the

hallway looking for the ice machine, stopped to ask a man if he knew where it was, then watched in open-mouthed amazement as the man faded into nothingness. There was also the case of a woman who stayed in Room 309 with her young daughter and found the child playing with an invisible companion.

"Don't you see him?" the puzzled little girl asked.

Ghost hunters and reporters galore have stayed in Room 309 and have emerged with stories of being pushed and pulled by an invisible entity.

"I feel as if Roger is still here, here in this room," one exclaimed excitedly.

Unfortunately, Roger was never in that room. Nor was he in either of the hotels from which the Horton Grand was built. Both were constructed after his murder. Whittaker—who liked to describe himself as a "dude"—was murdered at age thirty-seven by a fellow gambler and robbed of his money.

Perhaps because it is a relatively new property, investigations into the phenomena at the Horton Grand have been unusually thorough.

Whittaker is believed to have been hiding in an armoire when he was murdered, and there is an armoire in Room 309. Now guests have witnessed him floating down the staircase in nineteenth-century garb as a cold chill works through them. But he is not alone:

Deegan goes somewhat further and claims that while she was walking up the spiral staircase to the third floor, she once met a group of fifteen or twenty ghosts. She told a popular newspaper, "They were all dressed in the style of the 1890s and were having a dance."

Such claims, one might reckon, do little for the credibility of the Horton Grand's ghost story. There is also the fact that Roger the lodger is undoubtedly good for business. Offers to exorcise him have been turned down, and Room 309 has bookings for years to come.

"This," says Deegan, a trifle unnecessarily perhaps, "is a good place for ghosts."

The ghosts seem to be good for bringing in the customers, too.

Horton Grand Hotel
Address: 311 Island Ave., San Diego, CA 92101
Website: www.hortongrand.com

MENDOCINO HOTEL AND GARDEN SUITES
Mendocino, California

The Mendocino Hotel and Garden Suites is the only hotel remaining from a time when this was a booming port for the logging trade. The original structure of the hotel, dating from 1878, now contains the lobby bar, dining room, kitchen, and some of the upstairs guest bedrooms.

In a way, the hotel reflects much of Mendocino's history. Built at a time when the town had a population of twenty thousand, compared to one thousand today, it was known as the Temperance House—"the one good bastion of Christian morals in a town of loggers." Its fortunes then dipped until 1975, when it was bought by R. O. Peterson with the intention of restoring it as authentically as possible.

As a result of this restoration, the property now contains many treasures from around the world. There is an excellent dining room featuring period wallpaper and mirrors, original oil paintings, a massive English sideboard, and nineteenth-century glass screens from British railway stations. Wood paneling and stained-glass detail lend to the historic elegance.

There is a beautifully carved antique oak bar, set beneath a stained-glass dome, and a carefully tended Victorian garden. The fifty-one bedrooms and suites are all comfortably equipped with many boasting period-adjacent details such as four-poster beds and armoires.

Originally settled principally by New Englanders, the historic village of Mendocino looks like a coastal village in Maine. Pacific storms can fill the fields with fog, to give the surroundings a mysterious and romantic atmosphere. San Francisco is about a three-hour drive away; the region's plentiful wineries and spectacular redwoods are much closer, not to mention easily booked horseback riding and whale-watching adventures.

THE GHOSTS of the Mendocino Hotel are a series of mysterious figures that appear both in and around the hotel—but nobody can hazard a guess as to their identity. The only clue is that the town of Mendocino is a former fishing village on a particularly treacherous stretch of coast. Many fisherfolk have lost their lives in storms around here, so perhaps some of the victims and their loved ones remain in this otherwise lovely spot.

But the beautiful young woman, who appeared in the lounge and spent some moments gazing out the window before mysteriously disappearing, was no fisherman. Nor is the Victorian woman who haunts tables six and eight in the restaurant, where she appears in a mirror.

One-time front desk clerk Dorothy Pear-Green, who witnessed the former strange occurrence, explained:

"One night I had just stepped into the back office when I happened to look through the office window into the lounge. I saw a beautiful woman, with long blonde hair and beautifully dressed, standing in the lounge window gazing out onto the bay. She looked like an honest-to-goodness real person. I looked down for a moment to pick up some papers, and when I looked up again, she had gone. She certainly wasn't one of our guests: She was dressed in Edwardian style, almost Gibson-girl fashion."

Pear-Green has also heard voices calling "Dottie"—which was her childhood nickname and not known to anyone in the hotel. She says, "I would turn around expecting to see someone, but there was nobody there."

This said, she is quick to emphasize that since starting work at the hotel when it opened nine years ago, "I have had nothing but good experiences here."

The girls who make up the bedrooms, however, have several times reported making up the twin beds in Room 10, then going back with clean towels a few moments later and finding a body-shaped indentation on one of the beds. Dorothy Pear-Green, who slept in Room 10 as an experiment, recalled waking in the night and "felt this presence in the room—a sort of heaviness."

A recent Trip Advisor review reads "beautify hotel but haunted" before going on to warn of a hoarsely laughing spirit who not only taunted but appeared in the bathroom mirror. "I would not go there alone," the review continued before stating that nothing about the hotel's shared guest rooms denoted guests would be sharing with dead people. More happily, the reviewer raves about the "splendid breakfast." Which, happily, she enjoyed alone.

Mendocino Hotel and Garden Suites
Address: 45080 Main St., Mendocino, CA 95460
Website: www.mendocinohotel.com

NOYO HARBOR INN
Fort Bragg, California

Noyo Harbor Inn is perched on a bluff on a bend at the mouth of the Noyo River and stands in two acres of lushly landscaped grounds. Paths lead down to the busy harbor, where sea lions bark an exuberant welcome to the returning fishing boats.

A twin-gabled house, built for a lumber baron in 1868, the property has been remodeled with the most recent renovation opening on Christmas Day in 2017. This restoration was begun by Joseph Marino who employed the finest local materials and artisans to update the beautiful inn while retaining its original Craftsman touches.

The guest rooms and suites are beautiful. They all have private bathrooms, antique decorations, couches and chairs. Some rooms have fireplaces and adjoining sunrooms. Flexible cancellation fees and a dog-friendly environment add to guest's ease of mind.

There are lots to see and do in Fort Bragg, a charming little town. Beaches and state parks with hiking trails are practically on the doorstep. The famous Skunk Train ride into the redwoods is a top attraction, as are visits to the Botanical Gardens, museums, antique shops, and art galleries. Visitors can go horseback riding on the beach, while boats set off for fishing expeditions and whale-watching excursions from the docks just below Noyo Harbor Inn.

 THE GHOST—OR, RATHER, THE GHOSTS—at the Noyo Harbor Inn are a honeymoon couple who stayed in Room 5 in the 1940s. One evening after dinner, they set off for a drive up the coast—the man wearing distinctive light-colored clothing and his blonde bride in a red dress. They never came back, for they were both killed in an automobile accident near Grange Hall.

But in 1983, perhaps the young couple did return to the hotel where they had been so happy. One former owner, who was showing another couple around the hotel one day, was surprised when a young man wearing distinctive light-colored slacks and shirt and a girl in a red dress—both of them looking very pale—emerged from Room 5 and walked past the visitors on the landing and down the stairs. When he had finished showing the visitors around, and because he had not seen the other couple before, the former owner asked the restaurant manager, who had been standing at the foot of the stairs, where the two strangers had gone. But the restaurant manager insisted that no one had come down the stairs, and a check on the guest register showed Room 5 was empty.

Another former owner, who has since died, also reported disturbances involving Rooms 1 and 3. Doors opened and closed mysteriously. A human form sometimes appeared on freshly made beds. Once as he left the empty hotel, he also saw a girl in a white dress parting the curtains in Room 3 and staring down at him. When he went back inside the hotel to check, he found Room 3 deserted. But, on what was a very warm day, the room felt bitterly cold.

It seems as if the Noyo Harbor Inn ghosts play tag around the second-floor bedrooms. Room 5 is not the honeymoon suite and there are no stories to explain the girl in Room 3 or the phantom sleepers in Rooms 1 and 3. The hotel had recently changed hands at the time this book was being researched, and the new manager had not experienced anything out of the ordinary. But she did let me browse through the visitors' journals kept in each room, which tell the recent history of the hotel through guests' eyes.

Part of Room 3's journal was missing—allegedly destroyed by a guest who found a "frightening" story in it. And Room 5's journal recorded that, in 1988, a couple known only as Fred and Carol were moving to Room 4 "because of circumstances beyond our control." Mysteriously, they had made no entry in Room 4's journal, so that's where their story stopped. Could they have been a man in light-colored clothing and a blonde girl in a red dress?

Noyo Harbor Inn
Address: 500 Casa del Noyo, Fort Bragg, CA 95437
Website: www.noyoharborinn.com

QUEEN MARY
Long Beach, California

Once, she was the most famous oceangoing liner in the world. Now she is a unique hotel berthed permanently in Long Beach Harbor.

And, even if she will never sail the seven seas again, the giant RMS Queen Mary is maintaining her nearly a century-old tradition of entertaining guests in comfort and style.

The Queen Mary made her maiden voyage in 1936 and spent thirty-one years at sea. During that time she made 1,001 Atlantic crossings, logged more than three million miles, saw war service as a troopship, and carried more than two million passengers. Included in the National Register of Historic Places, she is the centerpiece of the Queen Mary Seaport attraction and, with her large, elegant staterooms and numerous restaurants and banquet rooms, a top-class hotel.

The guest bedrooms were once the liner's first-class staterooms and are full of customized woodwork and veneers, and plenty of 1930s-style art deco furniture.

Award-winning dining is just footsteps away at Sir Winston's, which offers fine Continental cuisine for luncheon or dinner as well as a Royal Sunday brunch, while the Observation Bar offers 1930s sophistication.

There are also fast-food outlets, boutiques, and souvenir shops on board the vast ship. To find your way around you can join one of the daily guided tours.

THE GHOSTS on board the Queen Mary are numerous and are backed up by plenty of eyewitness accounts. "Sightings, voices, and noises have been reported time and time again," hotel management admits. In fact, the hotel is so proud of their ghostly appeal they proudly show it. Voted in the Top 10 Most Haunted Places in America by *Time* magazine, no wonder they are so eager to please guests in pursuit of a supernatural getaway. There are many stories to loan to the Queen Mary's haunted lore. A check of the records showed an eighteen-year-old crewman had been crushed to death at that spot during a drill in 1966. Guests touring the ship have since seen a pale youth in naval uniform passing through Door 13.

Or how about the tour guide who, walking through the engine room at the end of the day, saw a bearded man in blue overalls coming up behind her. Knowing he wasn't on the staff, she waited to guide him to the exit. But before he reached her, he vanished.

One particularly haunted spot is the first-class pool, maybe the spookiest part of the ship. Tour guides have seen both a swimmer in a 1930s costume and a woman in 1960s clothing in the pool area, but both disappeared before they could be questioned. Security guards often hear voices and the sound of splashing coming from the pool; when they enter, they find it deserted. Particularly puzzling is the fact that the unseen revelers often leave wet footprints on the floor. The pool is kept empty.

The kitchens, the original third-class children's playroom (a toddler died there in 1946 and the sound of a child crying can still be heard), a couple of first-class suites, and the forward storage area are all said to be haunted. And who is the lovely woman, dressed in a simple white evening gown, who is dancing by herself in the shadows in the Queen's Saloon?

During the war, the Queen Mary served as a troopship. Repainted and christened the gray ghost, she was fast enough and powerful enough to outpace any German warship. With Hitler putting a huge price on her head, she had orders to stop for nothing. One day, performing a complicated zigzag pattern at sea, she sliced the British light cruiser Curacoa in half and, because she could not stop to pick them up, 338 of the Curacoa's crew drowned. One of the gray ghost's oddest ghost stories concerns that incident. Guests who want to experience these spooky specters for themselves will find no end of opportunities to commune with the beyond. Paranormal Tours are built into the hotel's proud haunted heritage. Twilight tours of the decks at night, not to mention séances are available for the bravest of heart. Or about a turn dining with the grand spirits and welcoming them to your table before they catch you unawares? Amateurs will love playing paranormal investigator on a group tour while those who want to combine the spooky with the spectacular will enjoy the views of the Paranormal Skywalk.

Queen Mary

Address: 1126 Queen's Hwy., Long Beach, CA 90802
Website: www.queenmary.com

THE HOLLYWOOD ROOSEVELT HOTEL
Hollywood, California

Situated right in the heart of Hollywood, the Hollywood Roosevelt Hotel is a stylish property built in 1927 as the centerpiece of the film world—a role it still fulfills. Always the place to see and be seen, it staged the first-ever Academy Awards ceremony in its Blossom Ballroom in 1929, and it has hosted a variety of major movie premieres and opening night galas since. Now the longest operating hotel in Los Angeles, it maintains the glamour of its auspicious Hollywood history.

Original features such as the classic Spanish revival–style exterior and the famous Blossom Room remained as they had always been. Hand-painted ceilings were restored; Spanish wrought-iron grilles were renovated.

Today the hotel features 335 beautifully appointed rooms, including twenty luxury suites including celebrity and movie themed suites. A garden setting bordering an Olympic-sized heated swimming pool, Jacuzzi, and the Tropicana Bar provides guests with a taste of the upscale lifestyle afforded its famous guests.

Hollywood's "Walk of Fame," where the big movie entertainers of the past and the present have their names engraved in stars on the sidewalk, is right outside the hotel on Hollywood Boulevard. The renowned Mann's Chinese Theater is also on the doorstep, and attractions such as Universal Studios, Disneyland, Beverly Hills, and the Hollywood Bowl are all within easy reach. Errol Flynn, Shirley Temple, Brad Pitt, and Angelina Jolie have all checked in to the Hollywood Roosevelt. But the real mystery surrounds the celebrities who haven't yet checked out.

THE GHOST at the Hollywood Roosevelt Hotel is Marilyn Monroe. She's joined there by Montgomery Clift and a number of other stars.

Property renovations seem to be the most popular times to disturb the spirits. At one point, the hotel's publicity material admitted, "Yes, this property is haunted. There are many ghosts and spirits we know about, and probably a lot more that we don't know."

The easiest to check out is in the Blossom Ballroom. Just two weeks before the hotel reopened after a renovation in the late 1980s, actor Alan Russell, working as personal assistant to the general manager, discovered a cool spot in the ballroom. Lots of staff and guests have experienced it, and it has even been investigated scientifically. It's a circle, about thirty inches in diameter. The temperature in the circle is about ten degrees cooler than the rest of the room. There is no obvious explanation for this and, although the cool spot dissipates when the room is crowded, it soon returns when the room is empty. Psychics say there is a man in black there, showing a lot of anxiety.

Former employee Suzanne Leonard had plenty of cause for anxiety herself on the same day Alan Russell discovered the cool spot. She was dusting the tall, dark-framed mirror in the general manager's office when she saw the reflection of a blonde girl in the glass. She turned around to speak to her, but there was no one there. Puzzled, Leonard reported the incident to her boss, who revealed that the mirror had once belonged to Marilyn Monroe and had been removed from the poolside suite Marilyn occupied at the hotel when the film star died. The mirror has now been moved to the lower-level elevator landing, so curious guests can keep their own lookout for Marilyn's ghost.

Stay at the hotel long enough and you could even cast your own film. Montgomery Clift, who spent three months in Room 928 while filming From Here to Eternity, has been felt brushing past people in the corridor outside the room where he once paced for hours, learning his lines. There's a "ghost writer" in the personnel office, who taps away at the electric typewriter after the empty office is locked up for the night; a lighting man who turns the lights on and off in Star Suite 1101/1102; and a sound man who makes telephone calls to the switchboard from empty rooms. There are even cast parties. Guests quite often call to complain about noisy neighbors in the room next door to theirs, only to be told the room is empty.

It would all make a thrilling film. But Montgomery Clift does not seem to welcome modern filmmakers to Room 928 and has caused all kinds of problems. Marilyn's mirror doesn't want to be filmed, and the cool spot in the ballroom is cold enough to affect audio equipment.

When research psychic Peter James spent some time investigating the hotel's phenomena, he felt the presence of numerous film stars: Carmen Miranda in a hallway on the third floor; Humphrey Bogart near the elevator; Errol Flynn, Edward Arnold, and Betty Grable in the Blossom Room; and Montgomery Clift up in Room 928.

The Roosevelt's Tropicana pool also attracts the haunting celebrities—who want to recline in style in their afterlife? Patti Negri, psychic and medium to the stars, told *Forbes* magazine that the energy around the pool and its fabulous artwork was "buzzy" with spirit energy.

So who needs to go to the movies? It's all there in the Hollywood Roosevelt Hotel, the stuff of which a publicity man's dreams are made. And, quite coincidentally, the hotel has felt moved to put out an eight-page press release detailing its phantom film stars and their latest personal appearances.

The Hollywood Roosevelt Hotel
Address: 7000 Hollywood Blvd., Los Angeles, CA 90028
Website: www.thehollywoodroosevelt.com

SCOTIA LODGE
Scotia, California

Located at the northern end of the Avenue of the Giants, where northern California's redwood trees seem to scrape the sky, the Scotia Inn is the original hotel for the town of Scotia—once owned in its entirety by the Pacific Lumber Company and one of the last remaining company towns in the United States.

The old hotel was torn down in 1923 and has been renovated several times since, including its current iteration "reimagined in 2021." As much a social club and hub as a place for transient travelers to rest, the lodge is nestled in the redwood mountains and near hiking, rivers, and vast wooded areas that will pique the interest of travelers. Twenty-two rooms and suites boast airy, modern appliances such as complimentary pour-over coffee and rapid charge receptacles so that your phone is ready to snap picturesque moments of your time in the redwoods or perhaps even to catch a ghost or two on the lodge grounds.

The Main and Mill Kitchen and Bar and its cozy craft cocktails, wood paneling and open spaces help marry the historic and the modern and act as a perfect hideaway to play a game of Scrabble or read.

Eureka is about a thirty-minute drive to the north, and San Francisco about five hours to the south. Locals will tell you to go hug a tree; it's supposed to be therapeutic. But, in these parts, you'll need a long reach.

THE GHOST at the Scotia Inn is called Frank. At least, that's one-time manager Hillary Carley said "He is very mischievous. He slams doors and turns lights off and on. He likes to scare people, but he is harmless. Just devilish.

"He follows women into the bathroom, then disappears when they get scared. He also gets people to follow him, thinking he is someone else, then disappears."

She believed the phantom prankster is the ghost of a man who committed suicide at the inn back in the 1950s. But that is not the only ghost the one-time manager encountered. A guest was alarmed to be awakened one night at about 3:00 a.m. by the sound of "a little girl, laughing and running down the hall in the hotel." Thinking she was their own daughter who had somehow clambered out of her cot, she checked, but found her still safely tucked up in bed, fast asleep.

Next morning they asked the manager if the child they'd heard in the hall was all right and discovered that their daughter was the only child staying in the inn. Hillary Carley reports, "Many people have heard this little girl many times, running merrily through the inn."

Recent guests also note haunted activity beyond feeling the presence of Frank on the top floor. A little boy sometimes plays ball while other guests report feeling watched, finding bedding disturbed, and hearing a lady who likes to hang out in the kitchen at night, muttering and laughing to herself.

Scotia Lodge
Address: 100 Mill St., Scotia, CA 95565
Website: www.scotia-lodge.com

US GRANT HOTEL
San Diego, California

When it was opened in 1910, it was hailed by the press as one of the premier grand hotels in the United States. And it still is. Exquisitely restored, the US Grant Hotel, built in honor of the Civil War hero and eighteenth president of the United States, Ulysses S. Grant, is now registered as a National Historic Site.

The 280 guest rooms are all presented in turn-of-the-century elegance—with two-poster beds, mahogany furnishings, armoires, and wingback chairs. They all have large bathrooms with marble and ceramic tile tubs. The suites offer built-in bars, and fireplaces with views of the downtown skyline and San Diego Bay.

The art-deco-designed Grant Grill is one of San Diego's most celebrated dining establishments with AAA and CAA Four Diamond Cuisine approval. Guests can enjoy seafood and a well-stocked wine cellar. For a slightly more casual experience, the Grant Grill Lounge is a favorite in the Gaslamp District for live music and craft beer.

An on-site spa and fitness center provide for guest's well-being. It is situated on the doorstep of San Diego's Gaslamp Quarter, right opposite the Horton Plaza shopping mall. San Diego Bay, the city's convention center, and tourist attractions such as Sea World and the famous San Diego Zoo are all within easy reach.

THE GHOST at the US Grant Hotel is Fannie Josephine Chaffee Grant, the first wife of Ulysses S. Grant Jr., who haunts a function room known as the Crystal Room.

Grant Jr.—known as "Buck"—and Fannie Chaffee were married in New York in 1880. Four years later, after the family had lost all their money in a scandalous brokerage firm failure, the Grants moved to San Diego. Fannie was having health problems.

They prospered in their new home. Grant became an assistant district attorney and his wife, whose family had made money from mining, land, and banking in Colorado, bought San Diego's first luxury hotel, the Horton House, in 1895. Ten years later the old hotel was demolished to make way for construction of the U S. Grant Hotel, which Grant planned as a homage to his late father.

But in 1909, before the new hotel was opened, Fannie died. Apparently unhappy that her husband remarried so soon after her husband's death, she takes it out by being a nuisance on the guests at his namesake hotel.

Since then, her spirit appears to have lingered on in the Crystal Room. She has been seen by employees and guests alike. Perhaps what makes Fannie unique from many of the other spirits in this collection is that she moves swiftly: maybe as spooked of you as you are of encountering her. Nevertheless, she continues to make her presence known. Room attendants have left cleaning supplies for split seconds only to turn to find them either missing or a long stretch from where they had placed them. Given Fannie's habit of roaming the hallways, guests can attest to chilly and cold corners of the otherwise heated corridors. But Fannie seems to have made some company: a recent guest spoke to lights turning off and on randomly and believes the fifth floor is also haunted. This new apparition seems to manifest in the shape of a stocky man with gray hair and a black suit who stands over the edge of the bed and watches guests as they sleep.

US Grant Hotel

Address: 326 Broadway, San Diego, CA 92101
Website: www.marriott.com/hotels/travel/
sanlc-the-us-grant-a-luxury-collection-hotel-san-diego

THE STANLEY HOTEL

Estes Park, Colorado

Nestled in beautiful Estes Park, the Stanley has a long history of providing guests with a restorative experience. The colonial-revival-styled hotel is at the entrance of Rocky Mountain National Park; the hotel was conceived by early twentieth-century inventor Freelan Oscar Stanley. Stanley heeded his doctor's medical opinion that a retreat to the Rockies' elevated heights would cure his resurgence of tuberculosis. After his recovery, he saw to the construction of the hotel and its surrounding district. While the main and surrounding buildings recall the architecture of New England, the surrounding mountains loan Estes Park and the Stanley a unique Colorado flair.

The Stanley Hotel is popular in media having been featured on *Top Chef* and in the films *Dumb and Dumber* and *The Shining*.

The Stanley Hotel features four distinctive types of accommodation: apartment-style rooms with kitchenettes, condo residences, the original historic rooms updated with modern conveniences and the boutique rooms of the lodge. Guests can enjoy the many indoor and outdoor sports and attractions of the nearby national park, musical events, and daily and nightly tours.

There are six restaurants within the Stanley Hotel's district including a whiskey bar and Cascade's boasting locally sourced and sustainable fare. While the hotel does not have air conditioning, it believes that the pure mountain air keeps it comfortable all year round with nature's remedy.

 THE GHOSTS of the Stanley Hotel are so numerous the hotel has designated spirit rooms renowned for their paranormal activity. Guests will want to book Rooms 217, 401, 407, or 408 to fully experience what is known as "Disneyland for ghosts." The hotel's haunted antics have been featured on the Travel Channel as well as *Ghost Hunters* on SyFy. The hotel is best associated as the macabre muse of horror legend Stephen King, who was inspired to write *The Shining* after a stay in the hotel. At the time of King's stay in the 1970s, the hotel had fallen on hard times and was in drastic need of repair, perhaps allowing the resident ghouls to seem more pronounced than usual. Room 217 is probably the most haunted, according to numerous articles and interviews about the Stanley. In 1911 housekeeper Mrs. Wilson was lighting lanterns in the guest room when she miraculously survived an explosion. To this day, she takes care of the room in her afterlife: recognizing her gratefulness for having survived long after her incident. Guests have documented their luggage being unpacked and objects being moved around the room in the order Mrs. Wilson prefers. Lights also turn on and off at whim.

But, be warned, Mrs. Wilson is rather old-fashioned, and unmarried guests have experienced the chill of an unwanted third bedmate intent on separating them.

Even if guests are not staying in one of the spirited rooms, the staircase between floors in the lobby area is known as "the Vortex." Here, the ghosts pass making visitors feel a chill even in the heat of summer or the sensation of someone walking through them all while Mr. and Mrs. Stanley might be seen watching from above.

The Stanley Hotel

Address: 333 E. Wonderview Ave., Estes Park, CO 80517
Website: www.stanleyhotel.com

BLACKBERRY RIVER INN

Norfolk, Connecticut

The Blackberry River Inn is a sprawling farm with a manor house dating to 1763. With access to over twenty wooded acres, guests are given the feeling of a broad estate. Inside the main house, dozens and dozens of windows, a cherry paneled library, hardwood floors and hearth fireplaces recall the rich history of the inn's earliest years. Guests can explore the grand entry foyer, the breakfast room, the music room and take local Harney & Sons tea and hot chocolate every afternoon in the library. The breakfast room is where a made-to-order breakfast (including the hotel's pride and joy—their homemade second-to-note waffle batter) is served daily.

The Blackberry River Inn is home to several rooms and suites in the main manor (with two hosting wood-burning fireplaces), and twelve deluxe rooms in the Carriage House and the Cottage; one large residence has a Jacuzzi tub.

In the summer, guests can recline near the outdoor pool and the vast grounds are always worth exploring. The Blackberry is perfect for travelers wanting to experience some of Connecticut's music and festivals with the Yale School of Music and Music Mountain and its summer concerts nearby. The Norfolk Farmer's market offers local, seasonal goods and Lee Premium Outlets is perfect for those who want to do a bit of shopping on the side.

 THE GHOST of the Blackberry River Inn is known as "Francis" or "the White Lady." One of the most haunted hotels in its state, the Blackberry River Inn is made more haunted by the vague details surrounding her residence. She is said to prefer haunting the inn's upper floor, though she often leaves the back entrance in search of an empty house behind. Could she be a figure as old as the Moseley House Farm (the inn's original identity)? Or, perhaps, she is historically linked to the ground's mysterious subterranean tunnels believed to be linked to the Underground Railroad. But guests record she is not there to scare or be mischievous. Rather, the feeling of a calm presence settles over those who encounter her as she slowly moves through the historic inn. Not everyone is as enamored by the presence of Francis, however. On one paranormal community site, a commentor is determined that the inn and surrounding area are so filled with a dark presence, he avoids walking or driving by altogether.

Blackberry River Inn

Address: 538 Greenwoods Rd. W., Norfolk, CT 06058
Website: www.blackberryriverinn.com

THE ADDY SEA HISTORIC OCEANFRONT INN

Bethany Beach, Delaware

This rustic and raised Victorian beach property was built by John M. Addy at the turn of the twentieth century. One of Bethany's earliest settlers, what had been intended as a summer retreat for his family, became a permanent residence. Now guests feel the old charm of the Addy from the moment they stroll up the sandy walkway to settle inn. There are twelve oceanfront rooms available for guests, including the Captain's Quarters with special amenities. Prospective visitors should note that the inn only accepts guests twenty-one and older. Once settled in the Addy, guests will enjoy rooms with spa tubs, in-room coffee and tea, and free Wi-Fi. A gourmet breakfast is provided every morning under a chandelier in the dining room and beach showers, chairs, and towels as well as a light lunch are provided for sea-dwelling visitors in the summer months. The wraparound porch with its many rocking chairs and waterfront views host the tea and treats served midafternoon. In the colder months, guests will find reprieve near the fireplaces in the parlor and dining rooms. Though the Addy does not have on-premises dining, it is within close walk of beachside restaurants and retail. For golfers, the Addy offers discounted stay and play packages with nearby Bear Trap Dunes.

Special events are taken seriously at the inn with everything from Babymoon to honeymoon packages available as add-ons.

THE GHOSTS of the Addy Sea Historic Oceanfront Inn are Paul Delaney and Kurty Addy. The former perished on-site at the Addy and may be partly responsible for the organ music heard at all times of day and night despite the fact that there is no organ on the premises. Guests who stay in Room 1 most often see or feel Paul. Kurty Addy has also long overstayed his original time at the Addy. Addy was working on the roof when he fell to his death years ago, but his footsteps are still heard nightly overhead.

According to visitors, Rooms 1, 6, and 11 are where the most paranormal activity and spirit energies are found. Room 11's bathroom, for one, is worth investigating alone: sometimes it shakes violently, other times the faucet turns on and off on its own.

The spirits may just become more restless the more the Addy shifts and changes. Though retaining its original nineteenth-century charm, the raised Addy has had to move several times over the past century and a bit. Nor'easters and dreadful sea storms have threatened and jostled the building—and its phantom inhabitants—but it still survives. And, so it seems, do its permanent invisible residents.

The Addy Sea Historic Oceanfront Inn

Address: 99 Ocean View Pkwy., Bethany Beach, DE 19930

Website: www.addysea.com

OMNI SHOREHAM HOTEL
Washington, DC

Perfectly located in the U.S. capital, the Omni Shoreham has a long history of hosting memorable dignitaries and musicians as well as inaugural balls—including that of Franklin D. Roosevelt.

Since its opening in the 1930s, the hotel has been deemed "the City's Grand Dame" thanks to architect Joseph Abel's hybrid of Renaissance-revival architecture with what were, at the time, modern art deco touches. In its early years, the Omni Shoreham Hotel shared its basement with C. V. Harlan's furniture factory, and Harlan, a master wood-carver, is responsible for many of the handmade furnishings throughout the guest rooms. For lovers of music, the Omni Shoreham's history includes memorable performances by Eartha Kitt, the Mamas & the Papas, and Aretha Franklin. The hotel's proximity to nearby Arlington as well as the heart of historic DC make it a popular place to welcome tourists and business travelers alike.

There are 834 guest rooms and suites with marble bathrooms, in-room safes, plush robes, and Wolfgang Puck–selected tea and coffee. There is a spa (by appointment only) as well as a hot tub and swimming pool for seasonal use. Guests can dine at Robert's Restaurant (home to the famous Omni Shoreham crab cakes) or at Marquee's Bar and Lounge. Morsel's offers pastries and coffee, and the Splash Pool Bar is perfect for summer poolside beverages and bites.

 THE GHOST of the Omni Shoreham Hotel is executive maid Julia Brown, also famous—or infamous—for Suite 870. This penthouse residence has a remarkable view of Rock Creek Park, the Arlington skyline, and even the grandeur of the Washington Monument stabbing the skyline.

But the suite has a long and morbid history that begins with Henry L. Doherty: a majority finance partner in the creation of the hotel who moved his family into the Suite 870 apartment not long after the hotel's opening. Along with the Dohertys, their executive maid Juliette or Julia Brown resided ready to keep the suite in tip-top shape and see to the family's every need.

Unfortunately, a few months after they moved in, Julia died in the night. Her body was discovered shortly after she called the front desk—presumably for medical help—the phone receiver still dangling from her hand. She placed her last call near 4:00 a.m. Several years after Brown's passing, Doherty's wife and daughter mysteriously died in the suite.

The expensive Persian rugs, the magnificent china once owned by Napoleon Bonaparte, the art and the furniture magnificently preserved in a static museum of an era long gone. Yet the harrowing history precluded anyone from wanting to stay.

To this day, the suite is carefully preserved and the public cannot merely reserve the suite. And while it is sometimes used to host dignitaries and guests, it remains—mostly—out of bounds. Perhaps out of respect, or as a cautious gesture. Yet, just because the suite is closed off, it doesn't mean that Juliette's influence isn't keenly felt by the hotel's other patrons. Guests often report a piano being played (there is no piano in Suite 870), and vacuuming as well as televisions flickering on and off at 4:00 a.m.: the time of the executive maid's death.

For those hankering after the harrowing and gruesome, perhaps the simple yet effective plaque on the door of Suite 870 reads: "GHOST SUITE."

Omni Shoreham Hotel

Address: 2500 Calvert St. NW, Washington, DC 20008
Website: www.omnihotels.com/hotels/washington-dc-shoreham

DON CESAR BEACH RESORT

St. Petersburg Beach, Florida

Florida's famous "pink palace" has towered over St. Petersburg Beach on the beautiful and still relatively uncrowded Gulf Coast since 1928. Known to its regular clients simply as "the Don," the Don CeSar Beach Resort retains its place as one of the leading holiday hotels in America.

F. Scott Fitzgerald, who was prepared to put his love for the Don on paper, referred to it as "the hotel in an island wilderness." St. Petersburg Beach has grown a bit since then—but it hasn't produced anything to match its most famous and most easily recognizable building.

Whatever you want on holiday, the Don probably has it. Especially now considering the recent renovation, "the Revival of the Don," named such to celebrate the hotel's near centenary and the commitment of the owners to continue to provide guests with an experience that blends its history with modern times. While the rooms and lobby bar are revived to host every contemporary luxury, the spirit of the Don's history is perhaps best found in one of its three main dining establishments, the Beacon. The Beacon is a double-decker pool bar that serves a wide variety of craft cocktails and seafood, but its starring location is where the real attraction lies. The Beacon lookout clocktower has a history as refined as the hotel itself: it has guided sailors home for almost one hundred years and in WWII housed watchmen scanning the gulf for enemy U-boats. Nearby, the Society Table nods to famous previous patrons Zelda and F. Scott Fitzgerald with its classic 1920s ambience. Finally, Uncle Andy's Market, redesigned as a 1950s ice cream parlor, is a great place to grab a cone or a grab n' go snack.

Outside facilities have been "revitalized" to match the sparkling interior of the wedding-cake hotel. Two swimming pools (one of them featuring underwater stereo sound) are surrounded by the multilevel boardwalk, and the new beach club and spa encourages personal fitness without too much in the way of strenuous activity.

The vast beach of white sand is right behind the hotel, and guided ecological walks along the shore are recommended. There's golf on the Isla del Sol. Other nearby attractions include the magnificent Salvador Dali Museum in St. Petersburg and the famous Busch Gardens. Day trips take in the rest of central Florida's famous family attractions.

THE GHOST at the Don CeSar is Thomas Rowe, who built the property in 1928 as a tribute to his true love, Lucinda, a Spanish opera singer. Some people say Lucinda can be seen there, too. Rowe had always promised Lucinda they would run away together and he would build her a pink Spanish castle with towers and rooftop balcony overlooking the sea. He kept his promise but sadly, Lucinda did not live to see it. Forbidden by her parents from continuing her association with Rowe after they met in London in the mid-1890s, she was taken back to Spain and the lovers never saw one another again.

Rowe's letters to the dark-eyed, raven-haired Lucinda were always returned unopened. Then one day a newspaper clipping announcing Lucinda's death was sent to Rowe at his home in New York, along with a final letter from his lover, asking him to forgive her parents. It reads, "We found each other before, and shall again. Time is infinite. I wait for you by our fountain to share our timeless love."

The letter—addressed to Rowe as "my beloved Don Cesar" (after the character in Wallace's light opera *Maritana*)—was signed "Maritana" (the role Lucinda had sung in London).

Shortly after this, Rowe moved to Florida on medical advice, and he began to build the pink palace he had promised Lucinda. The hotel took three years to build and, at $1.2 million, cost three times more than expected, largely because Rowe insisted that the lobby fountain be a replica of the one in the courtyard where he and Lucinda used to meet.

Rowe, famous for his light summer suits and panama hat, became a familiar local figure. But his hotel was not an immediate success. After Rowe collapsed and died of a heart attack in his beloved lobby in 1940, the property was drafted into duty as a WWII hospital.

It was not until 1972 that work began on renovating the property back into a luxury hotel. The work seemed to disturb the spirit of Rowe, for a panama-hatted figure was seen by construction workers in the lobby and in the corridors on the fifth floor where Rowe had once lived. Soon, hotel staff started seeing the figure, too.

Can you make a deal with a ghost? Yes, according to one-time public-relations adviser Lynn Peterson. Commenting on the fact that the phantom figure temporarily vanished from the hotel.

But while the panama-hatted phantom liked the offer initially, it seems he has backed out on the deal. Floor five seems to be where he enjoys taking residence: knocking or swinging doors open to aid room attendants with their arms full—perhaps proving he is still as hospitable as ever. And of course, he can be found strolling near the famed fountain in white suit and hat.

Perhaps Thomas Rowe and Lucinda have met one another once again by the fountain and walked out into the sunset together to find a timeless love.

Don CeSar Beach Resort
Address: 3400 Gulf Blvd., St. Petersburg Beach, FL 33706
Website: www.doncesar.com

HERLONG MANSION
Micanopy, Florida

Micanopy is known as one of the prettiest towns in Florida. It is "just oak and pecan trees draped with Spanish moss that shade a sleepy two-lane road to Old Florida's last stand," *Florida Trend* magazine once wrote. And the crown jewel in this pollution-free paragon of a place? The Herlong Mansion, says the magazine.

It is hard to disagree with that verdict. Begun in 1875 as a humble two-story house, the property grew along with the Herlong family's fortunes from timber and citrus. By 1915, times were good enough to build a classical-revival mansion on top of the original structure, complete with a Corinthian-columned frontage, and leaded glass and mahogany inlays galore.

Guests can look forward to a three-course homemade breakfast sourcing organic local produce, eggs and meat on a menu that rotates daily. Complimentary cookies and wine are also provided. Visitors are invited to lounge in the large living room and parlor where books and a board game library will inspire you to shut your phone off for a few blissful hours. (Though Wi-Fi is still readily available).

Micanopy is a quiet and romantic little place, its tree-canopied streets full of antique and curio shops. The Micanopy Museum, housed in the one-hundred-year-old Thrasher Warehouse, is within walking distance of the Herlong Mansion. It is a short drive to Cross Creek and the home of Marjorie Kinnan Rawlings, the Pulitzer Prize–winning author of *The Yearling*; or to the twenty-thousand-acre wildlife sanctuary of Payne's Prairie State Preserve. The family attractions of Orlando are about a two-hour drive away.

THE GHOST at the Herlong Mansion is Inez Herlong, the former owner of the house, who so loved the property that she sacrificed her family ties to do so.

The first people to "meet" Inez were a team of workmen brought into strip and varnish the floors in 1987. Because there was no electricity in the house, the crew slept in sleeping bags in the ground-floor parlor. Sometime between midnight and dawn they heard the door of a second-floor room open and close, followed by the sound of footsteps in the hall. Suspecting local hooligans, the workmen ran up to the hall—only to find it deserted.

Former innkeeper Sonny Howard believes the spirit the workmen heard was Inez, because she braved a lifelong family feud to own the house. Her mother left the property to be divided among her six children, but they quarreled about who should live there. Eventually, Inez Herlong Miller, who had also inherited money from her husband's estate, bought out her brothers and sisters after a two-year legal battle. She had won her beloved home, but she lost her family. None of them ever spoke to her again.

In her declining years, Inez was increasingly unable to look after the house properly. She collapsed and died while cleaning and polishing on the second floor. When her remains left the building, however, her spirit stayed on perhaps to help run the inn.

When ABC News and *Good Morning America* ran a Halloween feature on the uninvited woman often joining guests throughout their stay, they referred to her as "the woman in white." This moniker was taken from Jim Healey who volunteers at the nearby Micanopy Museum. Most of the guests who report Inez's presence feel her most keenly in the room she once occupied. A true Southern aristocrat, Inez's legacy could very well influence non-believers not in her manifested spirit but in the atmosphere of the refined mansion wherein she continues to reside with its grand columns and manicured gardens. Perhaps the peace Inez couldn't find in the midst of her familial battles has found her amid the columns and greenery of the renovated and refined estate.

Herlong Mansion

Address: 402 NE Cholokka Blvd., Micanopy, FL 32667
Website: www.herlong.com

Georgia

JEKYLL ISLAND
CLUB RESORT

Jekyll Island, Georgia

A playground on one of the Golden Isles off the coast of Georgia, Jekyll Island is a historic monument in its own right.

Constructed in 1886, the resort has grown continuously since its inception as a retreat for a select consortium of the nation's top businessmen, including such names as Astor, Rockefeller, Morgan, Vanderbilt, and Pulitzer. From its original clubhouse there sprang a village of apartment blocks and summer cottages. Alongside these "cottages"—in reality vast and luxurious mansions—are golf courses, marinas, and sports facilities of all kinds.

Today the Jekyll Island Club Resort retains the grand tradition begun in the closing years of the nineteenth century. It radiates an atmosphere of luxury, exclusivity, and excellent service, although today's visitors don't need the bank balance of a Rockefeller to be able to enjoy it all.

The public rooms and guest accommodations are of a Victorian elegance and offer every modern comfort. Boasting a curated coastal escape as well as fashioning itself as an "island sanctuary," it is the attention to detail that makes the Jekyll a premier spot for pampering. Just look at the many dining options, from the "bar on the pier," the Wharf, and its open-air dining featuring favorite Southern cuisine, to Eighty Ocean, which, in addition to a range of dining fare, offers a limited and casual pool menu for those choosing to lounge. The Pool House and the Pantry are perfect for guests who want to relax while the Grand Dining Room offers a taste of the opulence afforded guests in the resort's earliest days. A concierge can help you choose the best of amenities ranging from bike rentals to art and history tours and the "classical or casual" approach reflected in the dining offerings will apply to a range of perfect picnic baskets available to guests who want to explore the surrounding areas.

Surprisingly, the club's grounds also house its own historic district, where guests can investigate the original consortium's homes and the first owner's house, the 1824 DuBignon Cottage. Guests can visit the Rockefellers' cottage and other buildings including a museum and the 1904 chapel with its Tiffany glass—all fully furnished with original and period items.

The one-by-nine-mile island is linked by causeway to the mainland. Jacksonville and Savannah are both an easy excursion. The Okefenokee Swamp, with its rare and abundant wildlife, is practically on the doorstep.

THE GHOST at the Jekyll Island Club Hotel is Samuel Spencer, a guest at the club in the early 1900s. Spencer, president of the Southern Railroad Company, decided to join his fellow tycoons on vacation at the new and luxurious club on Jekyll Island. Enjoying the pampering that was—and still is—a hallmark of this extremely homey resort, Spencer developed his own routine for what became his annual stay.

He insisted on being accommodated in the "choice" apartment in the Clubhouse, an apartment with a vast marble fireplace, massive mahogany furniture, and a wide veranda offering open sea views. He also demanded that the *Wall Street Journal*, ironed smooth and folded just so, be delivered with his morning coffee. Only then could the railroad magnate settle in to enjoy his vacation amid the sea breezes of Jekyll Island.

This morning ritual continued happily for several years. Then one day in 1906, Spencer was killed in a crash between two of his own trains.

Ever since, guests occupying Spencer's preferred apartment have noticed several strange things that occur regularly each morning.

First, they find their morning paper folded differently, or opened at the business pages. Second, they find their morning coffee poured, or a full cup "sipped on," when no one else is nearby.

It seems that Samuel Spencer enjoyed his vacations here so much he still comes back. Staff reservationists are happy to point out Spencer's "choice" apartment to guests. Not everyone cares to have unseen hands helping themselves to coffee, even if it is in such an elegant and airy apartment as the one Samuel Spencer is reserving in perpetuity.

Jekyll Island Club Resort
Address: 371 Riverview Dr., Jekyll Island, GA 31527
Website: www.jekyllclub.com

THE MARSHALL HOUSE

Savannah, Georgia

The Marshall House in downtown historic Savannah is one of the South's most popular destinations. Built in 1851, the original owner was Mary Marshall who built it on property inherited by her cabinet-maker father. From 1864 to 1865, the house was converted into a hospital for Union Soldiers. It became an intermittent hospital several times throughout the nineteenth century during yellow fever epidemics.

Now the sixty-five rooms feature elegant period detailing and furniture, with recommendation to book either the spacious Mary Marshall suite or the Broughton Street Balcony room for the best views of the historic neighborhood. Located just a few blocks from the City Market and River Street, the Marshall House gives guests such a wonderful taste of antebellum Savannah on foot that many never unpark their cars.

The house offers its own type of museum with a third-floor Civil War–era art gallery and tours of the grand house and its wonderful stories that suit the ambience of the guest rooms. Many of the rooms feature claw-foot tubs and all offer comfy robes. Breakfast is served in the 45 Bistro restaurant and offers biscuits, bacon, and grits as well as the lighter fare of cereal and fruit. A wine reception is held early each evening in the house's library.

THE GHOSTS at the Marshall House are friendly if plentiful. The former is proudly boasted on the inn's website where they heartily promote their spirited friends. Featured numerous times of the Travel Channel, most of the spirits seem to be those of Union Soldiers who were admitted to the house when it was a makeshift hospital and never checked out. Often listed in the Top 10 Most Haunted Hotels in the United States in *USA Today* and *Huff Post*, the Marshall House encourages guests to embrace their ghost hunting sprit with the same energy they do the house's rich history. In the 1990s, workers found human remains under the floorboards leading to an immediate thought of a historic crime scene, though it was later determined they were the amputated remains of many unfortunate solider patients. As for the most haunted room? Room 306 apparently sources a lot of paranormal activity but that is not saying much considering how haunted the entire house is. Ghosts have been spotted in the halls and foyers, children's laughter and running steps are heard in the narrow corridors and faucets turn on and off. Some guests see patients of the yellow fever epidemics roaming the halls though an amputee soldier moaning for a surgeon seem to be the most often seen and felt. Other times an odd, horrid smell or just a "bad vibe" let staff and guests know that they are not alone. The cleaning staff is known to play upbeat music when attending to particularly paranormally active rooms in hopes of (at least temporarily) keeping them at bay.

The Marshall House

Address: 123 E. Broughton St., Savannah, GA 31401

Website: www.marshallhouse.com

RITZ-CARLTON KAPALUA

Kapalua, Maui, Hawaii

Most people agree that Maui is the most beautiful of the Hawaiian Islands, and the Ritz-Carlton Kapalua, a part of the superb Kapalua resort, is one of the most attractive hotels there. It would be hard to find somewhere better to stay. Especially considering the extensive range of dining and lounging experiences: from the cocktails and local sandwiches of the Olu Café to the vibrant Coastal Cuisine of Banyan Tree.

To one side of the hotel, the rugged peaks of the west Maui mountain range soar toward the sky. On the other side, the sparkling Pacific Ocean stretches toward the horizon. These, or the luxuriant gardens, form the view from all 492 guest rooms and fifty-eight suites. All the rooms come complete with every modern hotel convenience, ranging from round-the-clock room service to white marble bathrooms with plush terry bath robes. Slide open the shuttered doors of your room, and there is nothing to separate you from the gentle breezes of the white sand beach.

Sports facilities in the mild, year-round climate are superb. Golf on one or all of Kapalua's three famous courses; tennis (including floodlit courts), swimming, surfing, and snorkeling are popular. There's a fitness center in the hotel and a children's program.

Top sightseeing choices include hiking up the Haleakala Crater, helicopter trips, or whale-watching excursions from the nearby port of Lahaina, a historic town that offers good shopping and a lively nightlife.

THE GHOST at the Ritz-Carlton Kapalua hasn't been seen yet—but the potential is there. When excavation work prior to building the hotel began in December 1988, the planners' worst nightmare comes true. Building workers discovered the hotel was being erected right on top of an ancient Hawaiian burial ground, containing the graves of more than one thousand native Hawaiians.

After extensive negotiations between the developers, state officials, and native Hawaiian groups, the hotel was moved to another site, and the burial ground is now being preserved as a historic park.

According to some reports, this was not the first time such a thing has happened in the Hawaiian Islands. Another major hotel hit a similar problem but continued the building work. Now mysterious shadowy figures are seen in the corridors by some guests and staff at the (not surprisingly) anonymous hotel. Hopefully, the Ritz-Carlton Kapalua has done enough to escape similar visitations, and there are no stories of anything unusual so far. But stay tuned.

Ritz-Carlton Kapalua
Address: 1 Ritz-Carlton Dr., Kapalua, HI 96761
Website: www.ritzcarlton.com/en/hotels/kapalua-maui

Idaho

THE WHITE HORSE SALOON AND HOTEL

Spirit Lake, ID

Built in 1908, the White Horse Saloon and Hotel is still the tallest building in Spirit Lake and one of the oldest. The Saloon's original wood floors and bar give guests the feeling of stepping back in time to the town's heyday as a stop for panhandlers and surveyors, nomads and prospectors. For an added historical touch, the iron prison bars from the old Spirit Lake Jail separate the saloon from the hotel.

The Saloon—now called Messy's Bar and Grill—has one of the largest selections of Canadian beer across the border. The entertainment on-site includes pinball, pool, darts, Golden Tee golf and a jukebox. On fall weekends when the weather permits, guests are invited to the adjoining patio for a bonfire.

Eight recently refurbished guest rooms are available for booking. But even in this the White Horse is unique. Guests are subject to a self-check in process with a prearranged code and key though the saloon staff will help those who have difficulty figuring it out. Even though many rooms don't have elevator access, some do allow pets for a fee. A few of the rooms have a shared bathroom and guests can request a room with courtyard view of kitchenette. Few rooms have TVs loaning to the historical atmosphere of the old hotel.

Nearby Spirit Lake is the perfect spot for swimming, fishing, and kayaking, and hikers and cyclists rave about the nearby West and East Lake Trails. For family entertainment, check out the Silverwood Theme Park and the Tree to Tree Idaho Adventure Course.

 THE GHOST at the White Horse Saloon and Hotel is known mere as "Big Girl." She is a harmless spirit though sometimes is joined by other who make as much clangor as the juke box and antics in the saloon on a Saturday night. Big Girl is rumored to be a former hotel maid whose son was killed nearby while crossing the street. To this day, she keeps near the spot of his death, maybe in hopes of being with him again. But she is not alone: the town of former gamblers and panhandlers is full of characters who like to make their presence known. Apparitions pop up in hallways, dishes fly of their own accord and doors open and slam at whim. And if you are a solo diner in the saloon? You can expect company. You might not be able to see them, but they'll be there.

White Horse Saloon and Hotel
Address: 6248 W. Maine St., Spirit Lake, ID 83869
Website: www.thewhitehorsesaloon.com

THE CONGRESS PLAZA HOTEL

Chicago, IL

The Congress Plaza Hotel is situated on Michigan Avenue in the heart of Chicago. A Windy City icon since 1893, it has hosted celebrities, presidents and dignitaries since its doors were first opened. Indeed, the hotel's nickname is "Home of Presidents" for having housed Grover Cleveland, William McKinley, Teddy Roosevelt, and William Howard Taft. Each of the 871 guest rooms feature Wi-Fi, a large bathroom, and pillow-top beds. Many boast a lake-facing view. Guests can take advantage of the on-site barbershop and the marble-touched lobby and even build a package that includes a nightly stay and a full American Breakfast in the Gazebo Restaurant. For dining options, the Congress is home to Rafael's for more upscale dining as well as the Congress Lounge, which features craft cocktails and more casual fare.

THE GHOSTS of the Congress are as lively as the city's rich mob history. While Al Capone and the Ghost of Scarface roam the halls, it is Peg Leg Johnny guests most often encounter. Prone more to mischief than malevolence, Peg Leg flicks room lights on and off and creates havoc with electronics. Peg Leg apparently killed a man behind the hotel and has been rambunctious and noisy since.

There is also the gruesome history of a desperate mother who pushed her two children from the twelfth story. Elevators now have been prone to stop on the twelfth floor even without a guest pushing their button. To add to the haunted surroundings, the Congress also has a tie to H. H. Holmes, the infamous "Devil in the White City," and known as the US equivalent of Jack the Ripper. He was known to loiter around the hotel's lobby in search of new victims to lure to his murder castle during the time of the Chicago World's Fair.

For a more refined specter, the Congress Hotel's famous Gold Room has a lady ghost who whispers in your ear as you attend a wedding or reception in this spectacular room. Arches, murals, and ornate wall sconces make the Gold Room the perfect resting place for a woman to continue to find a worthy suitor.

The Congress Plaza Hotel

Address: 520 S. Michigan Ave., Chicago, IL 60605

Website: www.congresshotel.com

Indiana

STORY INN

Nashville, IN

The Village of Story was founded in 1851 with the grant of a land patent from then president Millard Fillmore to Dr. George Story. The patent can still be viewed at the inn. Soon, Story was the largest settlement in the area. At its prime, the village boasted two general stores, a church, a one-room schoolhouse, a grain mill, sawmill, slaughterhouse, post office, and blacksmith's forge: everything needed for a prosperous life in the late nineteenth and early twentieth centuries. And yet once the Great Depression hit, Story lost half its population.

The Story Inn is the perfect blend of rustic and modern. With fourteen rooms and cabins available, the inn prides itself on being a "distraction-free" zone as guests slip away from their daily rush and into a simpler time. As such, the only Wi-Fi on premises is found in the dining room and the tavern. There are not televisions in any of the rooms and the website warns of the spotty telephone service (while assuring guests can use the phone at the front desk if needed). In contrast to the cozy ramshackle charm of the inn's outside, the dining experiences inside are renowned throughout the Midwest. Guests can expect fine rotating prix-fixe menus with wine pairings and a break-fast menu. The Story Still Tavern offers a cookout experience in the summer months where guests can relax with a drink from their large selection. The nearby Barn and Mill are perfect for hosting parties and weddings and promise attendees a unique experience complete with the Story Inn appeal.

THE GHOST of the Story Inn is the Blue Lady. So often manifested within the walls, the room she frequents is known as the Blue Lady Room and located directly above the old general store. The blue lady was the wife of Dr. George Story. Her eyes have been described as "hypnotic" blue piercing through the dark when guests least expect it. She smells like cherry tobacco and she often leaves blue ribbons in the guest's rooms. Her lace gown swooshes underneath her as she impresses her memory so frequently the inn's guest books (not to mention Reddit threads and Trip Advisor reviews) are overrun with her sightings. There are accounts of doors opening and closing and a face appearing beyond one's reflection in the mirror. When a paranormal group brought electronic equipment, it was barely set up before it detected activity.

But beware and on your guard especially if you are staying in the Blue Lady Room. For flicking the blue night table light can stir up all manner of sightings.

Story Inn
Address: 6404 IN-135, Nashville, IN 47448
Website: www.storyinn.com

VILLISCA AXE MURDER HOUSE

(JOSIAH B. AND SARA MOORE HOUSE)

Villisca, Iowa

Josiah B. Moore purchased the Queen Anne house and its surrounding property in 1903. Just a decade later and two months after the sinking of the RMS *Titanic*, the murders of Moore, his wife, his four children and two-house guests were bludgeoned to death in their sleep. The horrific murders knocked the *Titanic* headlines from the front page for the first time in months. Investigators later found two spent cigarettes in the attic where the killer watched and waited until the family was asleep. All eight victims, including the children, bore severe head wounds with Josiah B's face bearing the worst. Evidence shows that after killing all of the family, the perpetrator returned to extend more blows to the elder Moores.

Every transient and unaccounted for stranger, including a

traveling minister, were questioned and suspect. The first trial ended in a hung jury and the second trial was never concluded leaving this one of the most terrifying unsolved crimes in American history. Ten years later, a similar axe murder took place and killed an entire family in Hinterkaifeck, Germany. The similarities between the two have posited many theories that the killer was one and the same.

Overnight tours are by reservation only and fit groups up to ten. Guests are encouraged to bring their own sleeping bags, blankets, and pillows and be prepared for minimal heating in winter months. Because the rooms have been perfectly restored to mimic the family's house at the time of their deaths, no candles or lanterns are allowed in case of fire: though flashlights and electronic lights are encouraged. Guests will find electricity and running water in the nearby barn.

The owners hope guests will ghost hunt and snap any audio or photograph evidence of their findings: they only hope that you will be generous to share your evidence with them!

 THE GHOSTS of the Josiah B. and Sara Moore House are the family, the two guests, and the couple's four children. For the latter, guests often bring toys and balls for the spirits of the children to play with and find them moved or gone with no explanation. Electric voice phenomenon systems (EVP), videos, and photographs determine this is one of the most haunted properties in Iowa or any state. According to one glowing review "This is a paranormal investigator's dream." While the house offers daytime tours, the ghosts are most often active during the midnight hours much as when they were peacefully sleeping before their horrendous murders took place. Podcasts such as My Favorite Murder, a 2016 film about the murders and several ghost adventures episodes prove that guests want to find the answers many believe the ghosts will eventually reveal: including the identity of their killer. Longtime tour guide Johnny Houser told the *Daily Iowan* that he was skeptical about ghosts when he first took the job fifteen years ago. That was until he was cleaning alone in the house and heard footsteps and a dresser door slamming upstairs. The noise was so loud, he suspected an intruder but when he rushed to the second floor to confront them, found he was completely alone.

He has since stayed in the house more than four hundred times in hopes of pinning down what has evaded so many: the sight of an actual ghost. Reporters and reviewers do often speak of disembodied voices having conversations in ethereally tones and rhythms that are undetectable to the living. Shadows have been caught on old cameras and rocking chairs move of their own volition.

This is probably the most violently gruesome property mentioned in the collection and as such has the most active paranormal activity and may continue to do so until the family finds either peace or the justice of knowing that their unsolved case has been solved.

Villisca Axe Murder House

Address: 508 E. 2nd St., Villisca, IA 50864

Website: www.villiscaiowa.com

HOTEL JOSEPHINE

Holton, Kansas

Founded in 1890 by A. D. Walker and named for his daughter, Josephine, the Hotel Josephine brings a blend of Victorian and modern to the storied history of the building. Current owner Sara Fox has restyled the hotel as a hybrid of the building's elegant first days but with convenient modern touches that promise a comfortable stay. The hotel's history—and former guest list—are impressive. Robert Louis Stevenson, author of *The Strange Case of Dr. Jekyll and Mr. Hyde*, former president Grover Cleveland, and temperance advocate Carrie Nation have all stayed in the hotel. The hotel also retains artifacts in memory of some of its famous lodgers including Carrie Nation's axe, Grover Cleveland's guest log signature and an original Campbell Football. There are seventeen rooms with two anticipated shortly after the time of publication of this guide. Hot breakfast is included in your stay and carriage rides and tickets to a yearly October haunted house can be purchased for an additional cost. Guests can dine at the Oak Roots Restaurant in the hotel and enjoy themed nights such as a family-style fried chicken dinner every Saturday evening. Horseback riding, visiting the museum, kayaking, and canoeing are some of the local attractions that the hotel staff can assist guests in booking.

THE GHOST of the Hotel Josephine is the eponymous daughter of the hotel's founder. Josephine enjoyed her namesake house so much she has yet to leave. In the downstairs parlor, guests will see that her graduation portrait is still hung above the piano. The prim, attractive young woman in high-collared Edwardian dress still watches from her picture and, apparently, many rooms throughout. Josephine likes to wander the corridors but is also fond of the basement.

The owners of the Hotel Josephine are determined that their inn is the most haunted in Kansas and as a feature of the largest international ghost hunt in fall 2021, they are clearly not alone in their assessment. Manager Tracer Fox began noticing paranormal activity during the hotel's most recent renovations. Portal mirrors, haunted dolls and paintings that moved were so startling that the hotel has even hosted a ghost-watching live stream. On his first overnight stay in the hotel, he awoke at 3:00 a.m. to the bed shaking violent. No wonder the PBS *PlainSpirits* series has featured the hotel!

Proud of their spirited heritage, the hotel's website features YouTube videos and pictures boasting the most haunted portions of the hotel and even skeptics would be hard-pressed not to notice the shadowy figures peeking clearly from otherwise blurry photographs. Perhaps because the hotel is so aware of its magnetic appeal to the afterlife, there are rules that restrict ghost hunters from access to certain parts of the house, from conjuring and provoking spirits and no Ouija boards are permitted on the premise.

The most haunted room is said to be the Buffalo Room and guests can specify their (brave) desire to stay in the room directly when booking on the hotel website. But even the Carrie Nation Room has had its fair share of phantoms. Several years ago, a woman hanged herself in the bathroom of the Nation Room. Guests who stay in the same room have been reported running out into the hallway, clutching their necks and unable to breathe.

For ghost watchers who want to find a community of kindred spirits, the activities and social media sites of the Hotel Josephine determine you'll find lots of ghostly activity on the premises or on the web from afar.

Hotel Josephine

Address: 501 Ohio Ave., Holton, KS 66436
Website: www.hoteljosephine1890.com

THE SIRE HOTEL

Lexington, Kentucky

The Sire Hotel dates back to 1916. But when it was constructed, it was not planned as a hotel—it was a hospital.

Inspired by the Mayo Clinic, three local doctors joined forces to erect the colonial-revival-style building that was to be the Lexington Clinic. It remained a hospital until 1958, when the clinic was moved into a new building. During its forty years of medical care, the old hospital had dealt with many strange cases, including one hardy patient who had a stick stuck in his eye for fifteen years, the painful result of trying to escape the tax men after he was caught distilling moonshine whiskey.

The old hospital became an engineering works for a while, then stood empty until it was converted into the new Gratz Park Inn in 1987. The inn has transitioned into the Sire, which is run by Hilton. Perfect for business travel, the Sire excels at providing guests everything they need for work or leisure.

Free parking, an outdoor terrace and a fire pit are just two of the hotel's amenities. Several bourbon bars and four-star restaurants are within walking distance to complete your stay.

The hotel is in the heart of Lexington's historical district and only three blocks from the business district. Shopping in Victorian Square is nearby. Local attractions such as the Keeneland racecourse, Red Mile Racetrack, Kentucky Horse Park, and the world-famous Bluegrass Thoroughbred horse farms are only a short drive from the Sire Hotel.

THE GHOSTS at the Sire Hotel are presumably inherited from the building's days as a hospital. They appeared immediately after the reopening in 1987. Diana Stevie, the hotel's director of sales and marketing at the time, takes up the story:

"Soon after we opened, a customer came up to the guest services desk, upset because there was a little girl on the second floor playing with her jacks in front of the elevator. When he called out to her, she laughed and ran around the corner. The guest followed her, to make sure she got to her room safely, but when he turned the corner, the little girl had vanished into thin air."

Hotel staff promptly christened the little girl "Anna." She makes frequent appearances in front of both staff and visitors.

"Guests often comment on the cute little girl upstairs dressed in Victorian clothing and ask if she is going to be in some sort of competition or play," Stevie says.

Anna laughs, sings, and plays with her dolls as well as her jacks. Often, she tries to play hide-and-seek with hotel employees.

"We will see her open a closet door and hide, but when we open the door, she has disappeared," Stevie says. "Then you'll hear her laughter ringing down the hall and see her skirt as she turns the corner. But, needless to say, when we chase after her, she's nowhere to be found." Stevie and other hotel employees reckon the more they play with Anna, the more the sightings increase.

"She is our most frequently seen resident," Stevie laughs.

Not quite so amusing is "John," a mischievous spirit who likes to awaken guests in the middle of the night by turning on the radio or TV sets at full volume.

"Sometimes you can even hear his laughter reverberating down the hallway after you," Stevie says. "John gives our guests quite a scare sometimes, but we know he is just having a good time."

There are more good times going on that visitors don't always appreciate. Guests on the third floor sometimes ring down to the front desk to complain of people pacing around in the room above theirs, or a loud party in progress. Staff must gently point out to such complainants that there isn't a room above theirs. The third floor is the hotel's top floor.

Most recently, guests have spotted different apparitions: including a lady in a white dress, a conclave of inebriated party goers and an elderly man who enjoys turning on the TV for no reason either day or night.

One other phantom sometimes wanders into the laundry room and just stands there without speaking, looking forlorn.

The Sire Hotel

Address: 120 W. Second St., Lexington, KY 40507

Website: www.gratz-park-inn.hotelslexingtonkentucky.com

T'FRERE'S HOUSE

Lafayette, Louisiana

T'Frere's House, built around 1890 by Oneziphore Comeaux, is now a luxuriously comfortable and highly atmospheric bed-and-breakfast.

With just three guest bedrooms, all with private baths, T'Frere's House offers a rather special *en famille* atmosphere. Its cypress walls and Cajun-style furnishings all reflect the care of recent owners to preserve the essence of Cajun culture and cuisine.

There's a broad veranda to rest on in the cool of the evening, enjoying a "T'Julep" and a selection of Cajun canapés. The gardens full of great oaks, a charming gazebo, and camellias in which to wander.

The kitchen still has the Comeaux family fireplace, though the comfortable sitting and dining rooms have been modernized over the years. Guest rooms are neat and homey with fresh chintzes and soft drapes. T'Frere's House is on the outskirts of Lafayette, "capital" of Louisiana's Cajun Country. The city itself houses the Acadian Village and a living history folk museum in the form of a typical bayou town of yesteryear. The Lafayette Museum has a special section celebrating the glamour and traditions of Mardi Gras. And there is a nature station devoted to the wildlife of the bayous.

 THE GHOST at T'Frere's House is Amelie. She seems to be a permanent resident at the old Comeaux house. The Moseleys, one-time owners, knew her as an old and trusted friend.

Amelie is a tiny woman, dressed in turn-of-the-century Cajun style. Peggy Moseley reported meeting her first on a summer's afternoon when she was surprised to find all her lingerie laid out neatly on the bed upstairs. Moseley and her housekeeper, Louella, had only just finished putting it all away in a chest in the downstairs hall.

Being new to the house at that time, Moseley resolutely put any fanciful thoughts from her mind. But a couple of weeks later, when she was alone in the house and telephoning a friend, she heard some terrifying crashes and splintering noises coming from the direction of the pantry. Dropping the telephone and running to investigate, Moseley found that something—or someone—had swept all the jars of preserves and other foodstuffs off the shelves to the stone floor, where they were smashed.

Moseley began to put two and two together. "I felt the house must contain something outside the sensory world," she reported. She began to be aware of something unseen about the house, a mischievous spirit who spoke French.

Undaunted, Peggy Moseley summoned a French-speaking friend and had him tell the empty air, "In God's name, I'll burn the house down if you misbehave." And she added, "Leave my children alone, leave me alone! And if you wish to go on living here, there are house rules!"

Peace prevailed, although Amelie, as the spirit came to be called, seemed to dislike hymns played on the piano. She splattered candle wax all over the keys and the polished lid whenever hymns were played—at times when there was no draft to account for the wax.

One of the Moseley's neighbors identified Amelie as an unhappy woman who had died in the house in an accident at the age of thirty-two. Moseley's mother saw Amelie in the garden, describing her as "a little Cajun lady, wearing her hair in a bun, dressed in a gown of ashes-of-roses color, with a cleft chin. She spoke French."

"A pity," said Peggy Moseley's mother. "She was so nice. I'd have liked to talk to her."

Amelie's mischievousness took a rather naughty turn at the wedding of the Moseley's daughter, Mary. The homemade punch, tasty and golden, suddenly turned a bilious green. On inquiry, it appeared that Amelie had been spotted in the kitchen, pouring liberal quantities of green food coloring into the punch bowl.

Amelie plays the piano and sits translucent in a rocker on the porch. She gazes down on visitors from an upstairs window and apparently causes mysterious green lights to rise through the hall floorboards.

Perhaps Amelie is trying to prevent the same fate befalling Peggy as had overtaken Amelie herself. The tiny Cajun woman drowned in the cistern at the back of the house while delirious with fever.

Amelie saved the whole family—and her former home—from devastation by fire. One night, the Moseleys awoke to find Amelie tugging at Peggy's arm and the room full of smoke. A fire had started in the dishwasher downstairs.

Peggy Moseley seems to think Amelie is merely lost.

While current proprietor Richard Young expounds on the theory in a more hallowed way. Young doesn't shy away from his property's history giving interviews and promoting it on the website. He believes that the Catholic Church's decision to rule her death a suicide. Not merely lost, Young believes she is "Caught somewhere in purgatory."

But, wherever Amelie is in time, she seems very closely tied to T'Frere's House.

T'Frere's House

Address: 1905 Verot School Rd., Lafayette, LA 70508
Website: www.tfrereshouse.com

LAFITTE GUEST HOUSE

New Orleans, Louisiana

At the far end of one of the most famous and storied streets in America the Lafitte Guest House, aka the Lafitte Hotel and Bar, suits the distinctive architecture of Bourbon Street well. The grand Old Easy motifs easily recognizable in layer-cake houses, wrought-iron balconies and awnings that *almost* waylay the heat ensure the Lafitte has its own brand of French Quarter magic.

Despite centuries of devastating hurricanes, the Lafitte has survived in many incarnations there to house guests attending a weekend wedding, Mardi Gras or a raucous bachelor or bachelorette weekend. The Lafitte has an on-site board as well as fourteen guest rooms, many with balconies overlooking Bourbon Street, and their website boasts a penchant for throwing amazing parties. There are fourteen guest rooms and a courtyard tucked away from the parties of the main street as well as a communal kitchen.

THE GHOST of the Lafitte is Marie, ten-year-old daughter of debt collector Paul Joseph Galieses, who lived there with her parents and five brothers and sisters before dying of yellow fever. Her mother, overtaken by grief, died in the same room (Room 21) years later. While the staff of the Lafitte Guest House won't outright confirm that Room 21 is haunted, they believe enough guest reports of strange occurrences have happened to keep them "curious," at least to the supposed goings-on in Room 21. But many wouldn't be surprised if more than little Marie inhabited the old guest house. The property on which the 1849 building stands now was once the San Carlos Hospital erected after a hurricane destroyed the previous hospital and perhaps many patients who perished there never fully left. The property was owned for several years by the notorious pirate Pierre Lafitte who had it built and furnished for one of his mistresses, Marie Villard: the mother of seven of his children, though they never wed. Marie, a striking mixed-race woman, was known as a "quadroon"; she was desirable enough to be seen on Pirate Pierre's arm as society companion but someone he would never wed. More still, Lafitte used Marie to shield his property from the law. Though Marie eventually purchased a house on Dumaine Street, there's a chance she still visits the home once shared with Lafitte, maybe out of frustration that her descendants, unable to hold office or vote, enlist in military service or marry whites were stamped by her love affair with Pierre Lafitte.

Lafitte Guest House

Address: 1003 Bourbon St., New Orleans, LA 70116
Website: www.lafitteguesthouse.com

CASTINE INN

Castine, Maine

This is a wonderful summer base for exploring the wild Atlantic coast-line of Maine: a bright and friendly inn, with a magnificently muraled dining room offering an equally magnificent menu.

The inn has practiced the art of hospitality since it was built in 1898. Guests arriving by car today are greeted just as warmly as those who once disembarked from boats at the town wharf (a mode of trans-port still chosen by some). A flower-filled front porch, someone to help with the bags, and a spot of iced tea are just the beginning of a wonderful experience that every inn should be imitating.

The maritime scenery of Penobscot Bay is justly famous, so it's fitting that many of the guest rooms offer sea views. The bedrooms, which include two suites, are furnished in the style of a cottage and have private bathrooms.

Guests of the Castine will enjoy one of nineteen guest rooms as well as a reasonably priced breakfast. Walk-ins are welcome. The Garden at Castine is renowned as one of Maine's finest featuring New England stonewall, specimen trees and a plethora of perennials. A mini-gym and sauna are available for guest use throughout their stay. Guests can also prepare to take the taste of the Castine home with them by purchasing some of the inn's locally produced jam. For those who want a curated adventure, the inn keeps a rotating list of specials on explorations that include kayaking and cycling along the coast. Children over the age of five are welcome, and overnight rates include a full breakfast.

There is a glimpse of the sea to be found in the dining room, too, although guests might find their eyes drawn to Margaret Parker's lovely murals. The menu features plenty of seafood, including local specialties such as steamed Maine lobster. Prices are extremely reasonable. Because the inn is licensed, wines are available to go with the meal. The inn also has its own pub.

Castine, perched on a seaside hill, is one of the prettiest towns in coastal Maine, with plenty of handsome nineteenth-century houses. The town square is one of the loveliest in New England, and the dark blue waters of the harbor are dotted with sailing ships.

Penobscot Bay windjammers often tie up at the town wharf. The Wilson Museum on Perkins Street helps set the local scene, and the forty-mile drive from Castine to Stonington is a scenic delight. Especially worth visiting is the Acadia National Park on Mount Desert Island.

 THE GHOST at the Castine Inn came as a bit of a surprise to the owners because the author seems to have known about it before one-time innkeepers Mark and Margaret Hodesh.

"This inn is not haunted," came the reply to initial inquiries. But the famous veteran British travel writer Kenneth Westcott-Jones and photographer Tony Hudson hold a different view.

"The Castine Inn is definitely haunted," Westcott-Jones says. "I am sure of that. It is the only place I've ever seen a ghost."

Westcott-Jones and Hudson were guests at the Castine Inn during the British general election in the early 1980s and stayed up very late waiting for the first results to come through on TV. Westcott-Jones was particularly interested to learn the result of the poll in his own outer-London constituency, but as the night dragged on without any news, he eventually went to bed and quickly fell asleep.

Sometime later, he awoke to see the shadowy figure of a man in his room. He recalls, "I thought it was Tony Hudson, with news of the election. I said, 'Who won Croydon North-East, Tony?' but the figure didn't reply. It just looked at me. Then I woke up properly and shouted, 'What the hell's going on?' and snapped on the bedside light. And the figure, who looked like an elderly man in waterproof clothing, just faded slowly away."

The phlegmatic Westcott-Jones went back to sleep, although he says, "I still didn't know the result in Croydon North-East." Next morning, feeling slightly bereft of both poll information and rest, Westcott-Jones questioned Tony Hudson, who assured him he had not been near the room or played any tricks. Wescott-Jones then reported the incident to a member of the inn's staff, who asked his room number (which he no longer recalls), then said unconcernedly, "Oh, that would have been the old fisherman."

If such nocturnal tales are the Hodeshes' idea of a nightmare, they have one consolation. Westcott-Jones and Hudson—who have both traveled very widely over the years—are insistent that the Castine Inn is one of the best places to stay in the entire region. While several decades have passed since these events, current locals believe that paranormal activity is not specific to the inn. Indeed, Castine itself is renowned for its paranormal activity—day or night.

Castine Inn
Address: 33 Main St., Castine, ME 04421
Website: www.castineinn.com

KENNEBUNK INN

Kennebunk, Maine

The Kennebunk Inn, built in 1799, has been welcoming travelers to historic Kennebunk Village since 1920, and the same standards of hospitality and service are offered to this day.

Open all year, this classic New England inn boasts seventeen rooms and six suites, all named for the first four U.S. presidents. Pet-friendly rooms can be booked upon requests and seasonal rates are worth looking into. There are also special rates for multi-stay nights and the inn welcomes business and wedding guests. But perhaps the distinguishing factor of the Kennebunk is its owners who list themselves both as innkeepers and chefs. Brian and Shanna O'Hea have appeared on *Chopped*, *Beat Bobby Flay*, and a myriad of other programs familiar to foodies. Featured on the 'O' Network, and the Food and Travel networks respectively, their approach to cuisine is as meticulous as their inn's hospitality. Guests will enjoy the chef's creative handling of the inn's extensive menu, which includes signature cocktails and an impressive wine selection.

Conveniently located in downtown Kennebunk, just ninety minutes from Boston, the inn is only minutes from the ocean.

Exploring Maine's famous seashore, mountains, and lakes is a favorite pastime for visitors. But there are museums, tennis, and golf nearby, and the inn is an ideal base for a spot of bargain hunting. Antique shops abound in Kennebunk itself, while the factory outlet shops in Freeport and Kittery are only a short drive away.

 THE GHOST at the Kennebunk Inn is believed to be Silas Perkins, a night watchman and auditor at the inn who was working there in the 1960s when he died of a heart attack. Silas was a well-known local character, who came from a sea-faring family and wrote excellent poetry in his spare time. When he died in his eighties, he was much mourned.

By all accounts he is still around, although some locals say it is an older ghost. A presence has been felt in the Kennebunk Inn's cellar. Someone plays pranks in the bar by occasionally causing mugs or glasses to levitate, and mischief has also been reported in Room 8. Staff readily admit that the inn is haunted. They're even proud of the fact that Kennebunk is listed as one of *Reader's Digest*'s Most Haunted Hotels.

The stories about Silas began when the former owners, Arthur and Angela LeBlanc, bought the inn, a transaction that, perhaps unwisely, they concluded on Friday the thirteenth. One of the first waitresses they hired refused to go down in the basement for supplies because, she said, she was psychic and a presence named Cyrus was down there.

"We pooh-poohed it and laughed," says Angela LeBlanc, "but she was very, very serious."

Then the LeBlancs heard the story of Silas and put two and two together (after all, "Cyrus" sounds like "Silas"). Silas confirmed the story by making three carved mugs levitate in the bar and crash into the back of the barman's head, an incident Angela LeBlanc might have found difficult to believe if she hadn't been in the bar when it happened.

"That kind of made a believer out of me," she says.

Since then, innkeepers Alex and Kathy Pratt have heard inexplicable banging noises, like someone knocking on a wall in the inn at night. Then Alex Pratt was in the bar with two other people when he saw someone walk into the restaurant. He went in to see who it was and found the room was empty.

"I even looked under the tablecloths," he says, "but there was no one hiding."

Perhaps he was wise not to ask too many questions. A waitress who boasted on her last night in the restaurant that the ghost "never got me" could only watch in amazement as a glass on her tray promptly rose into the air of its own accord, then smashed to the floor.

"If there's a spirit at the inn, it's nothing to worry about," Pratt says. "He's not a malignant presence."

No, but mischievous, maybe. He gets blamed for many things, including the embarrassing collapse of a honeymooning couple's bed in Room 8. A reporter from the *Boston Globe* who spent the night in that room found it an uneventful visit. But on the other hand, a group of amateur ghost hunters who made some tape recordings in the silent cellar were amazed to find later that their tape was full of mysterious ticking noises. So perhaps old Silas is still checking the books and composing the occasional ode in the silence of the long, dark nights.

Kennebunk Inn

Address: 45 Main St., Kennebunk, ME 04043
Website: www.thekennebunkinn.com

RANGELEY INN

Rangeley, Maine

Poised between the forests and mountains of Maine and the six Rangeley Lakes, the Rangeley Inn is a turn-of-the-century country inn with authentically restored rooms and antiques. It is open all year, catering to everyone from summer sun-seekers to winter sports enthusiasts. Despite Rangeley's relative solitude, it is a lively spot.

The rooms in the old building are attractive, and they all have private bathrooms. Some come complete with whirlpool baths and even open fireplaces. The lobby has a roaring fire in season, too. There is a large dining room, a lounge featuring live entertainment, and a veranda-style porch where guests can find a comfortable chair overlooking Main Street.

A TripAdvisor Traveler's Choice winner several years in a row as well as featured in Best of Maine magazine, the historic fireside bar and lounge offers numerous breakfast options for purchase—such as lobster benedict—as well as fare to unwind and indulge in after a day of fishing, birdwatching or waterfront explorations.

The Rangeley Inn knows how to keep the majority of its guests happy, especially from kayak and snow-shoe enthusiasts to winter skiers.

 THE GHOST at Rangeley Inn is Clarence. At least, that's the name that former innkeepers Fay and Ed Carpenter have given to the friendly spirit who seems to be around to help whenever there is a crisis.

Clarence first stepped in about twenty years ago when the Carpenters had just held an emergency meeting to decide how to deal with a staffing crisis in the kitchen. They came out of the meeting to find "a young lady standing in our kitchen. She looked like a hippie, with a long skirt of coarse fabric, boots, and long braid of hair. She seemed pleasant enough." The Carpenters were not quite sure how she had gotten into the house, let alone where she had come from. But she offered to wash up, was given a job, and remained at the inn for the rest of the season.

"While this incident was only a little surprising then, it was to be repeated time and again," say the Carpenters. "An urgent need, followed by the appearance of someone with the necessary skill to fill this need very capably, just in the nick of time."

Eventually, the Carpenters began to wonder whether they, or the inn, were being looked after by a sort of trainee guardian angel, like Clarence in *It's a Wonderful Life*. That's how Clarence got his name.

"We have decided it's Clarence who makes the floors squeak and the radiators sing at odd times, when the mood takes him," Ed Carpenter says. "We have tried to make him comfy, along with all our guests. In this case, though, Rangeley Inn appears to be his home."

The Carpenters add that their only regret is that Clarence is too shy to put in a public appearance. But he might have. Photographer Tony Hudson, on assignment in the lovely Rangeley Lakes region in 1984, had an odd experience in the small hours after the noise from some sort of celebration downstairs echoed in his room until 1:00 a.m.

Things quieted down, and he dozed off. Expecting to be called early to take photographs of a herd of moose at sunrise, he was awakened at 2:00 a.m. when somebody came into his room. At first, he thought it was the boatman. But when the figure didn't speak, he decided it must be a lost late-night reveler. He muttered, "Haven't you noisy blighters left yet?" The figure did leave by fading silently into the woodwork.

The Carpenters were unabashed by this incident. Indeed, they are still a trifle indignant that anyone should think caring Clarence would ever do such a thing to disturb a guest.

Rangeley Inn

Address: 2443 Main St., Rangeley, ME 04970

Website: www.therangeleyinn.com

THE BLUE MAX INN
BED AND BREAKFAST

Chesapeake City, Maryland

This comfortable bed-and-breakfast owes its name to author Jack Hunter, whose WWI flying saga *The Blue Max* has made thrilling reading and viewing for millions of people.

Hunter, a past owner of this delightful 1850s property, has one of the house's principal guest bedrooms named after him, a room of charm and distinction opening on to a private veranda.

It was this, and the other verandas of this Georgian federal home, that earned it the nickname "the house with generous porches." Whether overlooking the shady street or the pretty gardens, they make an ideal spot for relaxing. Innkeeper Christine Mullen's acquisition of the inn fulfilled a lifelong dream and the colonial and Georgian touches from paintings to color to furniture allow guests to relax in "affordable luxury." Guests can expect a full gourmet breakfast, fireplaces in most bedrooms as well as delightful little touches such as complimentary chocolate and beverages and specialty soaps and shampoos.

Chesapeake City—once logged on the map as "the Village of Bohemia"—is a center for water sports of all kinds. This is also horse country, and there are special tours of the area available for enthusiasts. If you prefer bargain hunting, then a visit to one of the two auction sales held locally each week is a must. Antique shops and ship and yacht watching are a favorite local pastime and the public dock ensures boating enthusiasts have easy access to the beautiful waterways.

THE GHOST at the Blue Max Inn is a Dr. Conrey, who lived at the house when it was still known by the name of the family who built it, the Lindseys (owners of the local sawmill). He now has a delightful room named after him at the inn.

Conrey's life was not all sunshine. His troubles—not documented, but apparently extreme—eventually overcame him. He committed suicide in his apartment on the third floor.

Since then, he has been sensed by many guests, and Christine Mullen herself, his spirit still occupying the rooms he made his own during his lifetime.

Perhaps, optimistically, the peace that evaded Conrey in life is found in his enjoying the hospitality of the Blue Max in the hereafter.

The Blue Max Inn Bed and Breakfast

Address: 300 Bohemia Ave., Chesapeake City, MD 21915

Website: www.bluemaxinn.com

THE CASTLE

Mount Savage, Maryland

There's a corner of the pretty little town of Mount Savage that is forever Scotland.

Some 150 years ago, Delano Roosevelt—an uncle of President Franklin D. Roosevelt—acquired the property as a base for his hobby: an ironworks (which later outgrew the estate and relocated to Pittsburgh). On the estate, Roosevelt built himself a replica of one of Scotland's picturesque stone castles, Craig Castle in the Highlands. Courting all seasons well, this spectacular house is a bed-and-breakfast set among richly planted, English-style gardens for the house is now refurbished in Scottish baronial style with many period items, original gas lighting, and massive gas fireplaces. The library and the great hall are atmospheric places to relax or dine. The six guest bedrooms— all bearing Scottish names—have handsome four-posters or a French Empire sleigh bed. Innkeepers Tony and Judi Perino welcome guests with sumptuous multi-course breakfasts as well as the added option of a private five-course dinner prepared by Tony himself. The four o'clock refreshment hour provides guests with an option of lemonade or wine to accompany sweets and cheeses. In the chilly winter months, a sit at the fire would not be complete without a specially prepared mug of whipped hot chocolate.

The Castle is set high in the mountains of western Maryland, amid wooded scenery reminiscent of Craig Castle's setting in the lochs and mountains of the Scottish Highlands. Excellent hiking terrain is all around, and there is a wide range of water sports. There are a number of ski centers nearby, too. Rather less energetic is the round-trip from Cumberland to Frostburg on the Allegheny scenic train, which runs May through December.

 THE GHOST at the Castle is of a Scotsman named Ramsay, a former owner. Ramsay arrived in Mount Savage in the early 1870s. Evidently wealthy, he bought the Castle and installed his family, glad to have found a spot so like his native land.

A brickmaker by trade, Ramsay produced the first glazed bricks in America. Indeed, he loved the feel of stone of all kinds, from marble to granite. Hankering for privacy, he surrounded the Castle with a massive stone wall in the style of the great Scottish estates. Inside, he created a beautiful garden filled with statues he had shipped in from Europe.

Ramsay's life in his new home was cozy until the Wall Street crash, when his fortune disappeared almost overnight. His brickworks failed, and the Castle was repossessed by the banks to pay off his debts.

In his rage at the turn his life had taken, Ramsay rushed out into his gardens with a hammer and smashed all his precious statues, toppling them into the dust the same way his own fortunes had been toppled by fickle fate.

The newly impoverished Ramsay was forced to take a job as an ordinary laborer in a ceramic's factory. Brokenhearted, he soon became ill and died. He and his wife now lie buried in Mount Savage Cemetery, in a vault made of Ramsay glazed bricks.

But former owners of the Castle, Bill and Andrea Myer, know just how hard it was for Ramsay to leave his "little bit of Scotland." In fact, they suspect that he never really did leave.

His footsteps echo around the empty third floor of the Castle, and the shadow of a man in a dark-colored frock coat has been seen there, as well as in the great hall and the library. Sometimes, according to Iron City paranormal website, he follows guests as they explore the stone mansion's grounds.

It is hard to dismiss this Scottish specter as "Scotch mist." Especially as recent guests record instances of a scratching noise coming from the Robert Burns room. The reports are so frequent, and so consistent, it seems certain Ramsay has settled back in his old home and intends to remain there forever.

The Castle

Address: 15925 Mount Savage Rd., Mount Savage, MD 21545
Website: www.castlebandb.com

KENT ISLAND RESORT

Stevensville, Maryland

Set among 226 acres of park and farmland on historic Kent Island Estates, beside the blue waters of Thompson Creek, stands the lovely white-columned house that is the Kent Island Resort

Once the "big house" for this waterside plantation, Kent Island Resort dates back to 1820 when it was the home of Alexander Thompson. Today, this gracious property is a flourishing hotel and restaurant where Sunday brunch in particular is a treat for locals and visitors alike.

Carefully restored to its early Victorian comfort and elegance, the inn has twenty-four guest bedrooms designed in the English Country style and a number of cozy lounges, some of which retain their original Italian marble fireplaces and window seats.

The house has verandas and a glassed-in solarium overlooking Thompson Creek. The extensive grounds include no less than one and a half miles of foreshore, and contain a number of marked paths and trails for joggers. Swimming, golf, corn hole, kayaking, cycling, a volleyball court and a firepit are available for summer guests. The Twin Creeks Café offers specialty cocktails, casual fare and a wide range of wine and craft beer options.

Nearby are a number of shopping malls, including antique shops, local crafts, and a factory outlet. There are several wildlife refuges within the radius of a few miles, and the big cities of Annapolis, Baltimore, and Washington, DC, are all within a leisurely hour's drive.

THE GHOST at Kent Manor Inn is that of Thompson himself: old Alexander Thompson, the original owner of the plantation back in the early 1800s. Thompson, after whom the nearby creek is named, was an extremely heavy smoker, so much so that he sometimes seemed to exist in a cloud of blue smoke.

His own bedroom, the room in which he died, is now Room 209. A century or so has passed since Thompson died, but Room 209 still carries a lingering scent of tobacco. No one is known to have smoked within its walls for years. Staff cannot eliminate the odor, no matter what they do.

Thompson seems to be the cause of some strange occurrences at the inn, too. Playful in life, he is playful still. Staff have reported being trapped in Room 209 by a table inexplicably pushed in front of the door. Lights flicker on and off for no apparent reason.

Thompson likes life to be lively. His tricks happen most often when the house is quiet. And it's when there are few people about and there is not much going on that a number of witnesses, including members of staff and two former owners, have reported seeing Thompson himself. On each occasion, he simply watches from a dim corner.

By contrast, he also enjoys a good wedding. The inn is a favorite place for celebrating marriages, and Thompson is often spotted at these ceremonies, joining in the fun as an extra, if intangible, guest.

Kent Island Resort
Address: 500 Kent Manor Dr., Stevensville, MD 21666
Website: www.kentmanor.com

COLONIAL INN

Concord, Massachusetts

Famous since 1716, when it was the home of one of Concord's first settlers, the Colonial Inn has become one of the town's most enduring landmarks. It overlooks historically rich Monument Square and has all the elegance of a former era.

The individually appointed guest rooms reflect the hotel's colonial style, yet offer such contemporary amenities. In the Main Inn, each room is individually styled and traditionally decorated. The Prescott Wing rooms have a cozy country charm.

A complimentary Starbucks coffee and a newspaper for each guest starts the day, and both of the inn's famed restaurants: Merchant's Row and the Liberty offer local fare (including lobster) and an enviable New England ambience.

The public areas of the inn feature several fireplaces, original woodwork, polished floors, and stacks of country charm. The main street of Concord is a delight of specialty wine, cheese, and antiques shops. For guests who want a spot of pampering during their Concord visit, the inn has a spa on premises.

The "two histories" of Concord come together to offer visitors a choice of things to see and do. There is ample Revolutionary War history at the Minute Man National Park, the Old North Bridge, and the Wright Tavern. Literary history comes to life in the Concord Museum, the Orchard House, the Old Manse, and the Wayside. For recreation in a historic setting, try boating or canoeing on the Concord River or swimming at Thoreau's Walden Pond.

 THE GHOST at the Colonial Inn is believed to be Dr. Joseph Minot, a Revolutionary War surgeon born in 1726 and a lifelong resident of Concord. He made his home in what is now the oldest part of the inn, which houses Room 24. It's there a blushing bride spent a very strange honeymoon night on June 14, 1966.

Nothing out of the ordinary had previously been reported by guests staying in Room 24, or for that matter anywhere else in the hotel. But newlywed Judith Fellenz, from Highland Falls, New York, awoke in the middle of the night with the feeling that, besides herself and her bridegroom, there was a third presence in the room. She opened her eyes and saw a grayish figure at the side of the bed.

"It was not a distinct person, but a shadowy mass in the shape of a standing figure," she said later. "It remained still for a moment, then slowly floated to the foot of the bed in front of the fireplace. After pausing for a few seconds, the apparition slowly melted away. It was a terrifying experience."

Mrs. Fellenz was too frightened to move, let alone wake her husband. Then, when she was able to move again, her fright turned to embarrassment. Nobody would believe she had seen a ghost, she thought. Her husband bore out that fear by teasing her when she mentioned it to him. So she kept quiet about the incident until, two weeks later, she wrote to the hotel to relate what had happened and ask if they had any explanation. The curtains in Room 24 had been closed, she said, so what she saw could not have been a reflection. She was fully awake at the time she saw the "extra guest" and "certain that it was not a figment of my imagination." Her letter, which was very detailed, added, "This sounds ridiculous, but I will swear to my dying day that I have seen a ghost in your lovely inn."

The innkeeper at the time, Loring Grimes, was not as disbelieving as Mrs. Fellenz had feared and wrote back to tell her the story of Dr. Minot. He also described Concord's connections with author and philosopher Ralph Waldo Emerson, and nature lover and writer Henry David Thoreau—two other candidates for the ghost in Room 24. Mrs. Fellenz and her army officer husband were invited to make a return visit to the inn, and they did. But they stayed in a different room and saw nothing.

Perhaps because the Fellenzes' story attracted some local press coverage, the ghost of Room 24 achieved a certain notoriety. Other guests began to describe strange experiences, and in 1986 a businesswoman from Virginia fled the hotel claiming she too had seen the ghost and would never again go anywhere near Room 24. In 1990, Mrs. Fellenz, by now remarried and going by the name of Cole, returned to the Colonial Inn—and Room 24—with her new husband, Bill. Although the shadowy figure did not reappear, the couple had a restless night.

"The room seemed to tease us," they said afterward. "There was something like an elusive beckoning."

Mrs. Cole added, "There is no doubt in my mind that a 'presence' has, indeed, attached itself to that beautiful corner room."

A local psychic who investigated the room in 1991 said it contained a benevolent male ghost who lingered there, not because of any special connection with Room 24, but because the inn was built over what had once been his lookout spot for guarding munitions. Later research disclosed that there had been a munitions dump opposite the hotel site in the early 1700s.

Also in 1991, a couple staying in Room 24 complained of being kept awake by repeated rapping noises on the inside of the adjoining bathroom door. The noises stopped whenever they went into the bathroom. But the couple were skeptics and refused to believe they might have had a visit from Minot. Many other unusual incidents that have been reported to hotel staff go unrecorded, says room sales manager Phyllis Dougherty.

As the Colonial Inn's fame has spread, so have the theories about the origins of the ghost. Emerson is a popular choice, because his family once owned the land where the inn now stands. Thoreau is known to have loved Concord dearly, so it is easy to imagine him being reluctant to leave. And Native Americans are not forgotten: One theory holds that the ghost is an angry woman from the Assabet tribe, who sold six square miles of land to the colonists so they could build Concord and who is now dissatisfied with the deal.

But no one will convince Carol McCabe that the ghost is anyone but Minot. On the night of December 9, 1994, he cured her stomachache.

Carol McCabe and her husband, Jim, who were staying in Room 24, had a large dinner that evening. Carol awoke at 2:45 a.m. with a stomachache. She went into the bathroom, got a glass of water, then went back to bed and lay on her stomach, "calling for the spirit of Dr. Minot."

Her SOS seems to have been answered. As Carol McCabe relates, "I suddenly felt a tingling sensation through my whole body. I felt as if electricity was going through me, and my body was rigid."

Unable to move, she could not look around to see what was

causing this, but when the sensation disappeared after a few seconds, she was able to look around.

"There was nothing in the room," she says.

Then the tingling sensation and partial paralysis began again, and after it was over it was repeated a third time. As the sensations grew weaker, Carol was able to relax and finally sleep.

"I can't help but wonder if Dr. Minot not only made his presence known to me, but somehow eased my stomachache," she says.

"Unsettling, but not unpleasant," is how Mrs. McCabe describes her experience. The most noteworthy thing about the unseen guest in Room 24 of the Colonial Inn seems to be that he seldom frightens visitors. Indeed, the room is the most popular in the hotel, and is usually booked up for months ahead.

"We do believe our ghost is a friendly spirit," Phyllis Dougherty says. "Nothing bad has ever happened."

Colonial Inn

Address: 48 Monument Sq., Concord, MA 01742
Website: www.concordscolonialinn.com

OMNI PARKER HOUSE

Boston, Massachusetts

Though renowned for its contribution to culinary history as the birthplace of Parker House rolls and the eponymous Boston Cream Pie, the Omni Parker House Hotel located at the corner of Tremont and School Streets at the crux of American Revolutionary history in Boston is rich in stories and specters.

The oldest continuously operating hotel in America since its original construction in 1855, the Parker is adjacent King's Chapel where the famous tolling bell recast by Paul Revere and Sons and the last one cast during the famous patriot's lifetime. Situated less than a block away, the Granary Burying Ground is the final resting place not only of Paul Revere but also John Hancock, Samuel Adams, and many members of Ben Franklin's family.

In walking distance of the Omni Parker, historical enthusiasts can visit what was once the site of bustling Scollay Square: a mecca of night clubs and bright marquises. A short walk opens up the world of the Common and the Public Gardens famous for their fountains and swan boats as well as the golden roof of the Massachusetts state building. In addition to the tolling bells at the neighboring King's Chapel, the Park Street Church, founded in 1804, towers over downtown Boston. The Parker House Hotel can also function as a starting point of the famous Freedom Trail, which will take tourists to the Old State House and the Old South Meeting House and down through Faneuil Hall in pursuit of the North End and the starting point of Revere's famous ride.

Guests can be guaranteed to experience much of the history that met some of the hotels most famous connecting historical personages. Ho Chi Minh, the Communist Vietnamese leader once worked as a baker in the kitchen. John Wilkes Booth, the actor turned assassin of Abraham Lincoln, was spotted at the hotel a mere eight days before the fateful night he ended the president's life at the Ford's Theatre in DC. For literary guests, the Parker once housed Mark Twain, is the meeting place of Newland Archer in Edith Wharton's *The Age of Innocence* and in *Death of a Salesman*, the eponymous salesman Willy Loman meets a client in its grand foyer.

THE GHOST of the Omni Parker House is Charles Dickens, author and creator of some of the most famous ghosts known to readers in his internationally popular *A Christmas Carol*, who stayed at the Parker on his second tour of America. A sensational literary celebrity on both sides of the Atlantic, Dickens had ignited the imaginations of American readers across the country. During his live performances, attendees were treated to real-life re-creations of the electrifying and vivid characters they had read about on the page. Renowned for embodying every last laugh and thrill, female audience members were recorded as swooning and fainting at a famous and grisly passage from *Oliver Twist* while men as enamored with the brandy and cigars of the portly Mr. Pickwick and his society would guffaw as their creator brought each comic vignette to life.

Legend has it that the mirror that captured Dickens's rehearsals captured far more. In fact, many believe the ghost of Dickens himself can appear not unlike the specter haunting Scrooge. Not surprising considering that the Parker is believed to be the most haunted hotel in Boston. Many believe that Dickens's ghost remains a writer in residence in the mezzanine that hosts the door and mirror that once belonged to Dickens's third-floor room before the reconstruction of the site in the 1920s. It's rumored if guests stare into the mirror long enough, Dickens in his full performance attire will appear. Others report that saying "Charles Dickens" thrice before their reflection in the mirror will hear the nearby elevator doors chime, even if there the mezzanine is deserted. If one is to be haunted, I can think of far worse phantoms than one of the greatest novelists of all time.

Omni Parker House

Address: 60 School St., Boston, MA 02108
Website: www.omnihotels.com/hotels/boston-parker-house

DEERFIELD INN

Deerfield, Massachusetts

Deerfield Inn, which was built in 1884, was remodeled in 1981 after a fire. It stands in what is called simply "the Street," described as the loveliest street in New England. It is now a full-service country inn, with twenty-four rooms between the main and carriage houses. Champney's Restaurant provides local and sustainable fare as well as a mahogany bar where guests can relax. Reasonably priced family packaged dinners for four are available to be picked up and taken back to guest rooms.

Old Deerfield is a national historic landmark. First settled in 1670, it witnessed the 1704 Indian massacre and the trials and tribulations of the American Revolution. Yet the eighteenth-century townscape seems untouched by the passage of time. No less than thirteen museum houses now line the street and encapsulate the cultural history, art, and craftsmanship of the Pioneer Valley.

There is a wonderful arts museum in nearby Williamstown. The historic villages of Shelburne Falls and Amherst are worth visiting, antique shopping is excellent, and country walks (to the old Native American lookout spot known as the Rock) and boating trips (to see the eagles at the Barton Cove) are recommended. In winter there is cross-country skiing in Northfield and downhill skiing on Mount Tom, both about a twenty-minute drive away. The nearby Norman Rockwell Museum as well as the Hancock Shaker Village.

THE GHOSTS—OR RATHER GHOSTS—at Deerfield Inn are those of a former owner, Cora Carlisle, and a rather mysterious, poltergeist-like apparition who goes by the name of Herschel. Cora Carlisle was a great believer in spiritualism. She used to hold séances in her living room; it has since been turned into a guest room bearing her name. The spirit she sought to contact was that of her husband, John. They had worked together closely on business matters during his lifetime, and Cora wished to continue consulting him about business. She called in a medium and believed she was successful in getting through to her late husband. Local historians say that the inn became a center for spiritualist activity.

Perhaps it still is, for occasionally Cora can be heard knocking on the door of her former living room and saying, "It's Cora, let me in," in an astringent and bossy voice. Present-day occupants who open the door and peep out might spot Cora in her nightclothes, moving off smartly down the corridor.

But Cora is quite well behaved compared to Herschel.

"Herschel likes to bother the guests in Room 148, the Chester Harding Room," innkeepers Jane Howard and Karl Sabo report. "We don't know why he's called Herschel. He's had that name before Lucille Henry, the receptionist, began working here, and she's been here for over thirty years."

There's no polite knocking on the door from Herschel.

"He slips under the door and appears in a bright box of light like a phone booth," the Sabos say. "The light breaks up and bounces around the room for a bit. If you are not paying attention by then, Herschel starts to tease by tugging at the bedclothes and lobbing magazines around the room."

A mysterious light source trying to remove the bedclothes would catch most people's attention. It proved a memorable experience for California surgeon Alan Tobias and his wife, Judith, when they vacationed in New England in May 1993. The locked door of Room 148 kept unlocking itself, static electricity cracked around the ceiling, magazines were thrown around, and the bedclothes kept being pulled off the bed.

Current staff believe the passel of ghosts are bossy and inquisitive, mischievous and cheeky rather than wishing ill will. For one, a front desk attendant reports a trick played on the "Owl Be Right Back" sign stationed at the desk. After returning from attending to a guest the sign had disappeared. An over-turned bowl of soup on way to a diner's table and a beaker of water crashing with no one around add to the spooky occurrences. But it isn't surprising considering Deerfield's reputation as the Oldest Ghost Town in Massachusetts. The main street's colonial charms are replaced by wandering spirits at night: perhaps most frequently at the Old Deerfield Burying Ground, which paranormal enthusiasts can indulge in before making a few deceased acquaintances of their own back at the inn.

Jane Howard and Karl Sabo are determined to mingle the past with modern conveniences. Inconveniently, it makes their ghosts feel as at home as the guests.

Deerfield Inn

Address: 81 Old Main St., Deerfield, MA 01342
Website: www.deerfieldinn.com

HAWTHORNE HOTEL

Salem, Massachusetts

Salem, a charming seaport on the coast of rural Massachusetts, is a town glowing with civic pride. Its seventeenth-century houses are beautifully preserved; its parks, gardens, old churches, and fine shops are all redolent of the gracious 1800s.

The Hawthorne Hotel is high-profile proof of Salem's civic sensitivity. It rose on a patch of land on the corner of Salem Common to become the focus of the town's hospitality activities. And it was funded by a highly unusual public subscription. Such funding is often a recipe for disaster or at best mediocrity. But this particular municipal building has avoided those pitfalls and earned its place among the nation's top hotels.

An atmospheric building dating from 1920, the Hawthorne is named for a famous son of Salem, author Nathaniel Hawthorne. The hotel prides itself on its exceptional warmth of welcome, its high degree of comfort, and its gracious hospitality.

As a base for following Salem's Heritage Trail, the hotel is perfectly placed. All the sights of Salem are within a few blocks—museums, churches, and other historical buildings reflecting the rather spooky Salem of the seventeenth century, when the town became notorious as the witch-hunting capital of the world. The delightful colonial city of Boston is on the doorstep, as is the lovely Massachusetts seashore. There are two dining options for guests: the Tavern, with its oak-paneled walls, burning fireplace, and seasonal martinis, is a perfect place to relax. Nathaniel's is alive with a 1920s vibe and offers prix-fixe

Sunday Jazz Brunches. Events such as a Santa Brunch and a Witch's Ball speak to the hotel's numerous yearly offerings. Guests will find complimentary newspapers and coffee in the lobby all year round.

 THE GHOST of the Hawthorne Hotel is no single specter. It is in fact the all-pervading atmosphere of those grim days in the 1690s when Salem Common—and the land on which the Hawthorne Hotel now stands—was the focus of the dreadful witch hunts that raged through this, the oldest continuous Protestant society in America.

The story is terrifying.

Through the influence of Tituba, a West Indian slave, the family of the Reverend Samuel Parris, of nearby Danvers, became notorious, and the local townships were rocked by hysteria and hate, strange phenomena, and accusations of devil worship and witchcraft.

The young girls of the Parris household were fascinated by Tituba's tales and giggled like any other young girls over the stories of love, death, and voodoo from her Caribbean home.

In the simple, God-fearing society of the time, any personal vanity, any simple pleasure such as dancing, any physical handicap, or even an irreverent sense of humor or a favorite pet, could be interpreted as an insult to the Lord. Cross your neighbor and you could find yourself denounced as consorting with Satan.

Malicious gossip, spiced with Tituba's gift for charms and love potions, and spiked by the overworked imaginations of a handful of teenagers, began what became a remorseless hunt to eradicate evil and the influence of the devil from Salem.

Neighbor was suspicious of neighbor; natural phenomena were misinterpreted and misreported; spite took a hand. First accused was

Rebecca Nurse, whose clapboard homestead still stands in Salem. Nurse was hanged, despite a petition by forty of her friends, many of whom later also stood condemned. Finally, an inquisitor was brought in to try the accused.

By the end of those dark days in 1692, almost 200 people had been accused and tried for witchcraft, 150 were jailed, and 19 died by hanging on Salem's Gallows Hill. One man, Giles Corey, refused to confess and died, pressed to death by great stones in an attempt to force him to recant.

"I petition to your honor," Mary Esty said, in her last words before being hanged in September 1692, "not for my own life, for I know I must die, but that no more innocent blood must be shed."

For all of Salem's bright, fresh paint, and flowers nowadays, there is a shadow still hanging over it. Salem's city fathers have carefully preserved as many records, buildings, and artifacts relating to this dark time as possible. The Salem Witch Museum is just one of the visitor attractions focusing on the witch trials.

The town is also known as the Halloween capital of the United States, with an annual festival celebrating everything that goes bump in the night.

But lest it seem as if the Salem of today has turned the tragic events of 1692 into a brash tourist attraction, it should be said that the town is at a focal point of much of America's early history. Its narrow lanes look much as they did in the seventeenth century. And it does have its own very special atmosphere.

At the time of publication, psychic medium and paranormal investigator Lucky Belcamino—a popular consultant to Stephen King's Hulu series and the Lizzie Borden House—was offering ghost hunts featuring the Hawthorne Hotel and several other of Salem's most ghastly haunted places.

Hawthorne Hotel
Address: 18 Washington Sq. W., Salem, MA 01970
Website: www.hawthornehotel.com

LONGFELLOW'S WAYSIDE INN

Sudbury, Massachusetts

———

The Wayside Inn, witness to almost three hundred years of American history, was initially a two-room dwelling on the Boston Post Road. It grew over the centuries to meet the demands of both the How family, who owned it, and travelers at a time when local laws dictated that an inn must "provide for a man, his horses, and his cattle."

For centuries, townspeople gathered at the inn to discuss the issues of the day. Here, too, Colonel Ezekiel How conferred with members of the Boston Committee of Safety and prepared for events that led to the birth of the United States.

Today's visitor to the Wayside Inn can enjoy the same peace and tranquility described by Henry Wadsworth Longfellow in the prelude to his poem *Tales of a Wayside Inn*. And the Hows' tradition of hospitality continues with magnificent New England fare.

After the publication of Longfellow's poem in 1863, describing the inn "built in the old colonial day, when man lived in a grander way," the inn became known as Longfellow's Wayside Inn. It is now a nonprofit and educational trust. The original trust was established by Henry Ford in 1946. After a disastrous fire in 1956, Longfellow's Wayside Inn was restored with a Ford Foundation grant. The inn is a National Historic Site, administered by an unpaid board of trustees. Revenue from the property helps pay for its upkeep and continuing restoration.

There are self-guided walking tours of the property, with its fourteen historic rooms and adjacent buildings, such as Ford's Martha-Mary Chapel and the Redstone Schoolhouse of "Mary Had a Little Lamb" fame. Boston is eleven miles away.

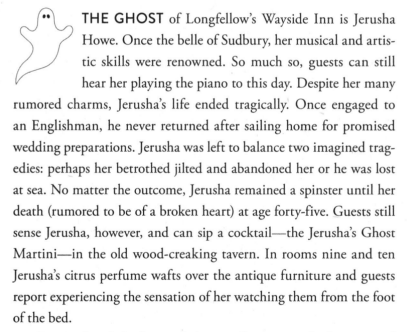

THE GHOST of Longfellow's Wayside Inn is Jerusha Howe. Once the belle of Sudbury, her musical and artistic skills were renowned. So much so, guests can still hear her playing the piano to this day. Despite her many rumored charms, Jerusha's life ended tragically. Once engaged to an Englishman, he never returned after sailing home for promised wedding preparations. Jerusha was left to balance two imagined tragedies: perhaps her betrothed jilted and abandoned her or he was lost at sea. No matter the outcome, Jerusha remained a spinster until her death (rumored to be of a broken heart) at age forty-five. Guests still sense Jerusha, however, and can sip a cocktail—the Jerusha's Ghost Martini—in the old wood-creaking tavern. In rooms nine and ten Jerusha's citrus perfume wafts over the antique furniture and guests report experiencing the sensation of her watching them from the foot of the bed.

Despite Jerusha's thwarted chance of romance, the longing and loyalty for her one-time love make her one of this collection's most bittersweet phantoms.

Longfellow's Wayside Inn
Address: 72 Wayside Inn Rd., Sudbury, MA 01776
Website: www.wayside.org

THE LIZZIE BORDEN HOUSE

Fall River, Massachusetts

One of the most unique bed-and-breakfasts in New England, the Lizzie Borden House is steeped in history. Lizzie herself is an American cultural icon and the subject of everything from an opera to a Lifetime movie starring Christina Ricci and an episode of the hit series *Supernatural*. Now the longtime museum of her house has expanded to let the bravest guests stay. The Lizzie Borden House has six rooms (including two in the basement) and provides guests with a glimpse of a "normal" day in the Borden household—including breakfast, which is included. Guests will dine on a modern interpretation of a meal Lizzie's parents ate the morning of their deaths. But the mutton and johnnycakes have been updated to pancakes, bacon, oatmeal, and fruit.

THE GHOSTS of the Lizzie Borden House are Lizzie's parents—Andrew and Abby Borden—infamous for their place in the trial surrounding their daughter grisly Lizzie and her "forty whacks" with an axe. They were both brutally killed on the morning of August 4, 1892, with many automatically pointing the finger at thirty-two-year-old spinster daughter Lizzie, who had, on record, tried to buy poison the previous day.

Guests with "ghost detector apps" have found that most of the paranormal activity is found in the "murder room" though guests note all bedrooms (each named for important figures in Lizzie's lore) are active with sinister energy. While Lizzie was acquitted of the crime of killing her parents, the trial was sensationalized enough to keep any spirit from truly resting in piece. So, Andrew and Abby continue to make their presence known, whether tugging on guests' clothing, opening and shutting doors, or just leaving enough of a chill in their wake that even those skeptic of the supernatural leave.

Or maybe the ghost is Lizzie herself, haunting the floor to atone while her cold and inconclusive case continues to baffle many.

The bed-and-breakfast doesn't shy from its gruesome heritage. They have plenty of Ouija boards available on premises for guest use, nightly ghost hunts, Victorian dinners, and mystery nights. While internet reviews for the hospitality and experience of the Lizzie Borden House are overwhelmingly positive, there does seem to be one area in which they are always graded poorly: sleep quality.

The Lizzie Borden House

Address: 230 2nd St., Fall River, MA 02721
Website: www.lizzie-borden.com

THE TERRACE INN

Petoskey, Michigan

First built in 1911 by proprietor's William J. and Josephine B. DeVol and their three daughters, the Terrace has served almost exclusively as an inn since its opening. There was a stretch during WWI when the inn was closed to tourists and opened as a hospital. There, volunteers cared for patients and rolled bandages for servicemen.

Today, the inn has thirty-eight rooms and suites, including the Garden Apartment Suite. This suite is a reasonably priced perfect solution for extended stays and once served as a tearoom called the Green Lantern in 1926. The other accommodations are a range of queen cottages and king suites (three of which have in-room whirlpools).

The 1911 Restaurant serves casual fare with a rotating seasonal menu. There is a happy hour of wine, beer, and small bites daily.

Guests of the Terrace Inn will find plenty of local things to see and do including the Maple Moon Sugarbush and Winery, which features maple flavored sweets and ice cream for the kids and wine tastings for the adult. The Petoskey Skyline Trail will cater to those with adventurous spirits and the Petoskey State Park is close at hand for all manner of exploration.

 THE GHOST at the Terrace Inn is believed to be Abbey Sweet who was in Room 211 when she suffered a miscarriage and died with her twins. It is this room that is said to be the hub of sensory effects and most often studied by psychics. Guests can specifically request the room, if they dare.

But Abbey is not alone; two workers killed by a beam while working on the construction of the hotel are also said to still haunt the premises. Yet the hotel encourages guests not to worry. The ghosts are friendly and harmless. They just haven't finished their occupation of one of Michigan's most beautiful inns.

The front desk keeps a twenty-five-year-old record of all guests' recordings of the strange and supernatural activities at the hotel. Perhaps guests who feel a chill of a presence, see the phantom outline of a woman roaming the halls near 2011, or even feel the strange sensation of someone accompanying them in an otherwise empty journey through the corridor can add their own account and thus be preserved in a long line of the hotel's haunted history.

The Terrace Inn
Address: 1549 Glendale Ave., Petoskey, MI 49770
Website: www.theterraceinn.com

THE PALMER HOUSE

Sauk Centre, Minnesota

The Palmer House is noted as living on the *original* Main Street. Its heritage and story interweave with that of famous author Sinclair Lewis. From the Palmer, guests are promised a taste and view of the bustle of authentic small-town life. The three-storied red-brick building occupies the corner of Sauk Centre's principal intersection. Its round arched windows and doors and decorative handwork recall the hotel's earliest days. And the extravagant touches—such as the stained glass imported from Vienna—speak to the original owner's determination to create a world-class experience in a small town. For in 1901, the Palmer was considered modern and avant-garde. It was the first hotel outside of the Twin Cities in Minnesota to have indoor plumbing. It was so memorable, Sinclair Lewis immortalized it as "Minniemashie House" in the 1920 American classic *Main Street*. Ralph and Christena founded the Palmer at the turn of the twentieth century to great success. Initially, the Palmer catered to traveling salesman arriving by rail (think Harold Hill in *The Music Man*) and promised a place to stay a night and a hot meal.

Today, the Palmer has nineteen rooms. Several contain Jacuzzis that are available upon request. Diners will want to check out the menus at the pub, which is stocked with craft cocktails and a daily happy hour. The kitchen ensures guests can dine in the restaurant or with meals delivered to their room. The website encourages each traveler to save room for dessert. Historical (and sometimes haunted) tours are available, and guests should consult the hotel calendar for details and dates. For golfers, the Palmer offers a stay and play package in conjunction with Greystone Golf Course.

 THE GHOSTS of the Palmer House are plentiful. Many checked in, but few checked out. But one is, to many, author Sinclair Lewis, who was hired (and fired) and hired again as a young man.

One reporter called the Palmer's basement "infamous" due to its paranormal activity and as only hotel guests are given access to the otherwise private floor, it is worth checking in as many of the transient guests-turned-phantoms have done over the decades. Because the ghosts inhabiting the Palmer are from all eras, guests could encounter an Edwardian-era lady or one of the business travelers who never made his final destination. One thing is for certain: the Palmer House is attractive enough to paranormal investigators find it a lively contrast to the town's wholesome, small-town image.

The Palmer has appeared on *Ghost Adventures* and *The Dead Files*.

On video, medium Aimie Allen confronted a presence attempting to physically control her. But the staff insist most of the ghosts are friendly. There have been no recorded deaths on the premises, and, unlike some of the other hotel histories in the collection, nothing sinister, gruesome, or macabre is recorded as having taken place between its walls.

According to a recent *CBS Minnesota* article, however, the owner insists that the Palmer "is never without unregistered guests." So guests continue to feel unearthly presences brush past them or call down to the front desk to complain about children running down the halls when the floors are otherwise empty of any family check-ins. Lights flicker and a snowman in seasonal storage starts to inexplicably dance.

But that's part of the fun. "Guests needn't hunt ghosts at the Palmer," owner Kelley Freese told local news. "You sit down and ask whoever is willing to come hang out with me, please do."

Who knows, you might even leave with an unexpected friend.

The Palmer House

Address: 500 Sinclair Lewis Ave., Sauk Centre, MN 56378

Website: www.thepalmerhousehotel.com

THE DUFF GREEN MANSION

Vicksburg, Mississippi

Built in 1856 by cotton broker Duff Green for his bride, the Palladian-style mansion was the center of antebellum-era entertaining in the Green's earliest years of residence. Green was such a magnanimous host that historical personages such as Jefferson Davis and Ulysses S. Grant were known to dance in the house's ballroom. Once Civil War broke out in 1863, Green saved lives and protected his house from Sherman's army by designating the mansion and the neighboring Episcopal Church as a hospital for both Union and Confederate soldiers. Locals credited him with saving the town. Guests can take a morning tour of the mansion and the nearby cave where the family hid during the siege and Duff's wife Mary gave birth to their first child. Inside, guests will be shaken by the bloodstained hardwood floors: one of the many stamps of the home's former life as a hospital.

Today, the Duff Green Mansion retains much of its former glory with its wide porches and Italianate-style iron railings. Instagrammers will want to snap every angle they can, especially in summer when the mansion is shaded by drooping magnolia trees.

Inside, all three stories feature furniture and antiques from the time period and each of the seven bedrooms will inspire guests to feel that they have stepped back to time. There are five ground-floor rooms and two upstairs suites, and some can accommodate pets upon request. Each morning, guests are served a three-course breakfast in a refined dining room under a grand chandelier recalling the Green's happier times at home. There is an outdoor pool and garden terrace where guests can recline. For those wishing to explore the area, the Yazoo River and the Coca-Cola Museum are within easy strolling distance.

THE GHOSTS of the Duff Green Mansion are plenty. Some guests recall seeing and sensing Little Annie, the Green's daughter who died at age six. Guests are welcome to stay in her former bedroom, but ghost hunters and former visitors warn that the mischievous little spirit has a dark streak. Unsurprisingly, one of the ghosts at the Green mansion is a Confederate soldier who rarely leaves his post by the fireplace in the kitchen where the amputations and operations took place when the mansion was a hospital. Guests record hearing his rocking chair squeak and even seeing his specter in uniform as they wander through. When a team from A&E's *Ghost Hunters* arrived, they sensed a lot of paranormal activity, guided by a former owner of the inn who had his fill of spirit beings during his tenure there. There are moans and cries that echo through the kitchen-turned-hospital. This doesn't shock most paranormal investigators, though, at one point the bodies of deceased soldiers became so overwhelming, they took up near every space of the ground floor.

The Duff Green Mansion

Address: 1114 1st E. St., Vicksburg, MS 39180
Website: www.duffgreenmansion.com

THE LEMP MANSION

St. Louis, Missouri

This Gilded Age mansion was finished in 1890 for Charles Lemp a German immigrant turned grocer turned Falstaff Brewery Baron and his wife, Lillian, and his children.

Though it has lived several lives, including that of a 1950s boarding house and though time and renovations have stripped the historic building, the current owners have ensured that there are touches of the elegance that would have met Charles and Lillian at the end of every busy work day as his brewery overtook five blocks adjacent the house (they eventually built tunnels to connect the two) and his beer became the first to be nationally distributed before the beginning of the Prohibition era.

Guests will be treated to original touches of marble, an ornately hand-painted parlor ceiling as well as etched and carved mahogany mantels. Each of the four suites feature touches in homage to the Lemp family including authentic chandeliers, rich carpeting, and furniture from their Gilded Age world.

The Lemp Mansion restaurant is rated with raves on almost every travel website and is as popular a dining destination with locals as with guests. On Sundays, an all-you-can-eat family-style dinner is served. Each guest will leave with a complimentary tote bag filled with snacks.

All reservations are prepaid and Wi-Fi and water are included. Guests will want to check the schedule ahead of time to ensure that they stay when the hotel hosts one of its mystery-theater dinners. There are daytime historic tours and overnight haunted tours of the house.

 THE GHOSTS at the Lemp Mansion are the four members of the Lemp family who committed suicide in the mansion. When Charles Lemp's son Frederick took his life at the age of twenty-eight, Lemp Sr. began to wane in mental health and was dispassionate about his ragingly successful brewery. After three years of decline, he shot himself in 1904. William Jr. took over the brewery after his father's and brother's deaths but he, too, committed suicide in the same manner of his father not long after. Finally, Lemp's daughter Elsa, who married into an abusive relationship, took her own life just as her father and brothers had.

Guests complain of ghostly knocks and phantom footsteps throughout the house. Contractors who worked on the restoration of the property complained of tools disappearing. Glasses left on the bar fly across the room and lights turn themselves on. The very tragedy of the Baron and his family's demise is enough to make many guests feel oppressed within the walls of this home of hallowed history. Indeed, *CNN Travel* not only marked the Lemp Mansion as one of the 10 Spookiest Places in America but in the world. The *Ghost Hunters* travel series has investigated the paranormal activity and the supposition that Elsa's death was a murder framed as a suicide is the subject of the feature film *The Case for Elsa Lemp*, which premiered in St. Louis in 2020.

No matter what guests take away from their time in the hotel— whether a ghostly video or photograph as a souvenir—the lesson of the wealthy family that "you can't take it with you" echoes through the mansion. But so does the age-old motto "money can't buy you happiness." It certainly didn't for the unfortunate Lemps.

The Lemp Mansion
Address: 3322 DeMenil Pl., St. Louis, MO 63118
Website: www.lempmansion.com

CHICO HOT SPRINGS RESORT AND DAY SPA

Pray, Montana

The stars of Montana shine bright over the century-old Chico Hot Springs Resort and Day Spa. Stars of stage and screen come in droves to dine, dance, and even sing along at this renowned western hideaway. Nestling at the foot of Emigrant Peak, among low sage-covered hills, this inn is in real cowboy country.

The Yellowstone Paver runs right beside the property, a long, low, white-framed building where show-biz luminaries such as Jane Fonda, Jeff Bridges, and Dennis Quaid have been known to come and "chill out." With all that national park wilderness on the doorstep, it's not surprising that guests at the lodge bring hearty appetites with them—the historic dining room offers a full breakfast buffet as well as a gourmet dinner prepared by a James Beard nominated chef. The restaurant also features one of Montana's finest wine selections. For dessert, the lodge's famous "flaming orange" has been indulging guests since 1974.

This old inn has guest accommodations in regular rooms, chalets, log cabins, condos, or even motel units, all furnished in a rustic cowboy style, but with every modern comfort. The hot springs are available all day and into the night for guest enjoyment and day passes allow for visitors to join them.

The lodge is the focus for myriad outdoor activities in the area. Everything from hiking and riding to river-rafting and skiing is available within an hour or so's drive. The battlefields of the Native American wars are hereabouts, too, such as Little Big Horn, and there are a number of Native American settlements to visit, ghost towns and gold mines galore. The breathtaking scenery of Glacier and Yellowstone National Parks is on the doorstep.

 THE GHOST at Chico Hot Springs Resort and Day Spa is Percie, a real gal of the golden West.

Percie arrived in Chico from Canada in the late 1880s to territory at that time, and life being hard in general, Percie decided to make it her home.

Already in love with the sage-covered hills, she soon fell in love with pioneer Bill Knowles. Together they built the Hot Springs Resort, ran the accommodations at the lodge, and created the celebrated restaurant, health spa, and resort facilities.

All this took time. Before the resort achieved its deserved fame, it had taken its toll on Bill's health. He died in 1910, leaving the grieving and courageous Percie to keep the resort going through good times and bad. In the worst of the depression it proved too much for her. Percie "retired" to Room 349 where she spent her time rocking in her chair, enjoying the magnificent view of Emigrant Peak, and reading her Bible. She died in 1940.

Percie's old room on the third floor still has her rocker. No matter how it is left in the room, it is always found facing the vista of the Absaroka Mountains and the commanding Emigrant Peak.

Percie's Bible was placed in the attic, away from meddling fingers. When staff have occasion to go up there, they check to see if it's safe. And they report the Bible is always found open, never a film of dust on its pages.

Another great character of Percie's time, and one fundamental to the success of the Chico Hot Springs Resort's health facilities, was Doc Townsend, an old-fashioned country doctor recruited by Percie to put the spa and its treatment center on the map. He did just that in the early years of this century, while coping with everything from attacks of biliousness to brain surgery.

When Doc died, the lamp he kept burning in his office twenty-four hours a day went dark. It has defied every effort to relight it since then.

Chico Hot Springs Resort and Day Spa
Address: 163 Chico Rd., Pray, MT 59065
Website: www.chicohotsprings.com

GARNET GHOST TOWN COTTAGES
Granite County, Montana

For a get-away-from-it-all vacation, stay in one of the cabins in the Garnet Ghost Town.

Back in the 1870s, Garnet was a real-life gold-rush boomtown—bustling, busy, and brash. Its name came from the semiprecious stones, a profitable by-product of the gold mines. Garnets can sometimes be found in the old spoil heaps, even today.

Like all boomtowns, Garnet was eventually hit by the inevitable slump. Gold fever moved on, the settlement declined, its population dwindled, and by the 1930s, the town had all but died. Now it has been brought to life by the Federal Bureau of Land Management and the Garnet Preservation Association. It has developed into a popular summer visitor destination. Its general store, saloon, and stables are as lively and as rowdy as they were in the town's heyday. Two refurbished guest cabins are available via a lottery system to visitors who want to "sleep with the ghosts."

One, known as "the Newlyweds' Cottage," was built by Mr. Davies, the successful owner of the Garnet General Store. Whenever he heard of a young couple in the town hindered from marriage because they couldn't afford a place to live, he would lend them this shack free of charge.

Winter access is limited to snowmobile or cross-country skis. The nearest all-weather vehicular road is ten miles away. Bearmouth and Potomac are the nearest villages, while Missoula some twenty miles distant is the nearest big town. Unique to many of the other hotels in this collection, the Garnet Ghost Town's amenities include rodent-proof cans, snow shovels, and firewood and axe in lieu of scented soaps and in-room Keurig machines.

 THE GHOST of Garnet Ghost Town is the spirit of the old mining town itself. Looking at the old clapboard settlement nowadays, it is hard to imagine it in its heyday around the turn of the century. Garnet was one of the most affluent gold-mining towns of the region, attracting sharp businessmen, tough miners, gaudy ladies, and earnest, hopeful settlers.

Today, Garnet sleeps through the deep Montana winters under a blanket of timeless snow. But in summer it springs to life, populated by characters from the good and bad old days. Desperadoes pop up at the saloon, covered wagons roll down Main Street, and gunfights erupt outside the Assay Office in a series of live, action-packed shows.

Ghost hunters claim Kelly's Saloon the most haunted with music and laughter whistling through the wooden slats of the historic building.

At the end of every day, when all the costumed characters and their props are accounted for, there is always a shadowy figure left on the sidewalk—a bewhiskered old-timer, a somber gunslinger, or a girl in a poke bonnet and homespun frock. The spirits stay on where they've always been.

Garnet Ghost Town may be dead, but it sure won't lie down.

Garnet Ghost Town Cottages

Address: Granite County, MT (see website for directions)
Website: www.garnetghosttown.org

MURRAY HOTEL

Livingston, Montana

There's a great party atmosphere at the Murray. Somehow this town-center property has a sparkle about it, whether or not there is any special function or holiday program in progress.

The hotel opened its doors in 1904, when it was known as the Elite Hotel, and immediately its ambience attracted movie moguls, magnates, and madcap personalities of all kinds. Situated at one of the crossroads cities in Montana, the Murray was often "on the way" to and from the West Coast for characters as diverse as movie director Sam Peckinpah—who actually listed the Murray as one of his homes—and the late Queen of Denmark.

Guests at the Murray can expect discounts for multi-night stays in the winter months. The hotel was featured in a recent TCM original documentary. Twenty-five rooms and suites each boast a distinctive style and there is plenty of on-site dining as well as recommendations for nearby. Gil's Goods Café, 2nd Street Bistro, and Murray's Bar are the options on-site: the latter renowned as the hub of Livingston nightlife.

Livingston is at the heart of Yellowstone country. World-class fishing, hiking, river-rafting, hunting, golf, and skiing are within an easy hour's drive of the hotel. And it is set among some of the nation's loveliest scenery.

 TWO GHOSTS at the Murray Hotel are lovely young women often seen and heard around the hotel and both of slight figure. One seen especially in Room 202 is wearing a glittering white evening dress. The other is only a faint wistful shadow on the fourth floor.

Both girls arrived at the Murray (then called the Elite Hotel) to enjoy some good times with Walter Hill, son of railroad magnate J. J. Hill. Walter Hill was smitten by the hotel on his first visit and retained a number of apartments in the old Elite on a long-term basis. He brought hordes of friends along with him to enjoy the grand balls and other frivolities for which the Elite was famous.

On one occasion, Hill was accompanied by humorist Will Rogers. So delighted were they with the warm welcome they received, they determined to share the experience with anyone and everyone. Full of high spirits and abundant bonhomie, the two madcaps added to the guest list a favorite saddle horse, which they took up to Rogers's suite on the third floor—via the 1905-vintage hand-cranked Otis elevator!

It was impossible to keep track of Hill's guests, whether invited or gate-crashers. After one such shindig, the two good-time girls somehow stayed on.

The younger of the two, only around sixteen years of age at the time, fell madly in love with Hill, although he did not seem to care much for her. She followed him around like a puppy. He grew so weary of her clinging company that he virtually banished her to her rooms on the fourth floor and forgot about her.

One day, staff reported she was no longer there. Had she checked out? They couldn't say.

What happened to this dazzled girl on the fourth floor, no one knows. But since then, staff and visitors staying in what were her rooms have experienced a number of strange phenomena.

Former hotel owners Dan and Kathleen Kaul have heard giggles. And once, telling a former owner proudly about the redecoration they had carried out on the fourth floor, they were startled to find the former proprietor becoming agitated, asking whether any of the walls had been stripped or replastered. When the Kauls asked why, the answer came, "If you plaster over the walls, she will not be able to come out."

Is there still a grim secret somewhere behind the fight partition walls of the fourth floor? Could it be that this young girl was ousted by Hill in favor of the girl in the long white gown? Certainly, this second girl, one of Hill's long-standing amours, often stayed in the hotel in Room 202. Her slender, glittering ghost is often seen moving through what was her room, along the corridors, and down the stairs en route to the ballroom, on her way to a dance that ended almost ninety years ago.

Walter Hill certainly knew how to throw a party. And perhaps still does. Staff remark on being uneasy to go down to the basement with its coal chutes and early nineteenth-century Otis elevator.

While one guest attested to seeing a man in old-fashioned clothes hovering by the bed. It seems that Walter's high times at the Livingston may not be over just yet.

Murray Hotel

Address: 201 W. Park St., Livingston, MT 59047

Website: www.murrayhotel.com

ARROW HOTEL

Broken Bow, Nebraska

The Arrow Hotel is definitely a modern take on the Old West. As soon as you enter the foyer, you are met with wood-paneled ceilings, oversized leather couches, hanging chandeliers and russet red detailing that recalls the spirit of its 1928 opening. Just off the city square and near the Custer County Museum, the Boneyard Creation Museum, and Melham Park as well as Broken Bow's small-town charm, guests will find plenty to keep themselves occupied.

The Arrow hosts twenty-four suites and rooms, some with private balconies upon request. Pet friendly and featuring a hot buffet breakfast, the Arrow also offers complimentary guest laundry, free Wi-Fi, cable with HBO, in-room coffee, and a fitness center.

Though the Arrow has undergone many identities during its almost century in business, it has always functioned as a hotel and dining room and the on-site restaurant the Bonfire honors the age-old traditions as well as offers a range of classic American fare.

THE GHOST of the Arrow Hotel is rumored to be a red-haired woman, believed to be a witch, and subjected to a brutal death. Though she is thought to be buried at the nearby Township Cemetery, guests and employees believe that her spirit has been at the hotel for years. Furniture moves on its own accord and apparitions appear out of nowhere as well as low whispered voices. Some think the red-haired woman has company as a former owner who died in the hotel likes to pace the stairs from the kitchen or sit in the cigar room.

For guests who want to meet a few other spirits, Broken Bow itself is listed as one of Nebraska's most haunted small towns. Spirits haunt the gazebo and roam the main streets. The local library seems to host more than books: it is said that voices float through the walls with no one on the other side. At the very least, they are whispers.

Arrow Hotel

Address: 509 S. Ave., Broken Bow, NE 68822
Website: www.arrowhotel.com

GOLD HILL HOTEL
AND SALOON

Virginia City, Nevada

Originally known as the Vesey's Hotel, the Gold Hill Hotel and Saloon is one of the few old buildings remaining in Virginia City's adjoining sister city, Gold Hill. Construction began in 1859, the same year a major gold deposit was found in Gold Canyon. Within a year, this region had become the world's wealthiest mining district.

The old stone part of the hotel is original and came complete with banqueting hall and saloon. But, when the Gold Rush faded, so did the hotel's fortunes. It became a miners' bunkhouse, then a private residence, before being restored and expanded into the luxurious country inn it is today.

The character of the old building remains. Inside the original stone walls, guests are transported back in time. All accommodations are decorated with period antiques capturing the unique flavor of the Comstock gold rush.

The 136-year-old Gold Hill Hotel and Saloon, the oldest hotel in

Nevada, is a link to the days of the Comstock Lode, the Silver Rush that came hard on the heels of California's Gold Rush. Miners and adventurers followed California's rivers back toward their source, panning for gold as they went in the hope of finding the lode of precious metal. They found one source in nearby Gold Canyon, but as they struggled to recover it, they cursed Gold Hill's sticky blue mud, which slowed them down and gummed up their machinery. Then they found the heavy blue mud was rich in silver.

So Gold Hill became a silver hill and turned Virginia City into a boomtown. And in 1859 the Gold Hill Hotel and Saloon was built to cater to the miners and millionaires, prospectors, and gamblers who flocked into town.

Now it proudly owns its heritage as a popular saloon with on-site dining and hospitality aware that it is the only full-service hotel in the Virginia City are.

Guests have a range of rooms for their stay including a miner's cabin, or the two oldest and original rooms, which are available upon request. As for dining, the Saloon, with its exposed-brick interior and slanting lean-to feeling of a roof, is equally warm near the fire in winter and the perfect patio spot in the summer. Themes like "Miner Mondays" offer guests a trip to the past.

 THE GHOST of the Gold Hill Hotel and Saloon is Rosie whom an old attendant described as "an old-fashioned looking gal with long reddish hair a white blouse and a long skirt." Nobody knows who she really was other than a lady of the night and perhaps her moniker comes from the strong scent of roses guests perceive when her spirit is near. Rosie isn't cruelly spirited, rather mischievous and guests who opt to stay in her room

(Room 4) will most likely encounter her. There is also a ghost named William who occupies the room next door (Room 5). Guests who opt to request these rooms are notified that their rudimentary lodgings make for an almost-certain encounter.

Due to the hotel's proximity to the Yellow Jacket Mine, ghosts from a widespread 1869 fire have never truly found peace. The fire burned eight hundred feet below ground level and killed more than thirty-five miners. The hauntings of the miners are trapped near the right entrance of the hotel. Ghost hunters keen on Nevada locations and paranormal investigators determined to find the most haunted corners of the country are adamant that the Gold Hill Hotel and Saloon is the place to encounter an apparition or two.

Gold Hill Hotel and Saloon

Address: 1540 Main St., Virginia City, NV 89440
Website: www.goldhillhotel.net

OMNI MOUNT WASHINGTON RESORT

Bretton Woods, New Hampshire

The Omni Mount Washington Resort is a spectacle that overtakes much of the Bretton Woods. The resort's surrounding mountain slopes and heavily wooded acreage ensure it courts every season well. Built in 1900 by Joseph Stickney who made his fortune in Philadelphia coal investments, the resort was well ahead of its time when it first opened to guests in 1902. Its steel frame structure, indoor heating and electricity were well ahead of its day. Stickney employed over 250 Italian artisans to see to the stucco masonry of the exterior granite while Tiffany stained-glassed windows rounded out his vision. Sadly, Stickney died of a heart attack not long after his resort opened.

Today, the resort is a popular destination for tourists and business conferences. Guests have a large selection of 269 suites and rooms to choose from—many boasting private balconies and patios. There is an on-site full-service spa, post office, and retail shopping. But it is the outdoor activities that attract many visitors well over a century after Stickney's time.

Named one of the best ski resorts in the U.S. and Canada, Omni Mt. Washington resort is ideal for arctic and Nordic skiing. In the summer months, an eighteen-hole golf course, red clay tennis courts, swimming pools, horseback riding, cycling, mountain biking, and hiking the many surrounding trails keep guests busy outside while the arcade and game room keep indoor guests occupied.

Dining at the resort offers a wide selection, from the century-old main dining room, to Stickney's Restaurant, which acts as a pub and steakhouse. For small bites, guests might pop into the Cave: the best place to catch the game on TV. The Rosebrook Bar features craft cocktails and spectacular mountain views. Seasonally, the Observatory Bar is the perfect outdoor reprieve.

 THE GHOST of the Omni Mount Washington is, surprisingly, not Stickney himself, having suffered a shocking heart attack on premises, but rather his widow, Carolyn. His young wife, though devastated by her husband's death, remarried Prince Lucinge of France a few years later and relocated to Europe until his death. Upon the death of her second husband, she returned to the Mount Washington, taking up residence at Stickney's grand resort and frequented a nearby chapel (still standing) where she would visit and pray for her husband's soul. Room 314 has apparently been haunted since Carolyn's death in 1936. An ethereal, elegant woman is often seen roaming the hallways near the room. To add, guests have captured her visage on photographs. Many spirit-seekers believe that the residence of Carolyn's actual bed in the room loans to its haunted presence. One Trip Advisor was disgruntled that he and his young family were not warned about Room 314 before booking. He records that the fireplace turned itself on, lights flicked on and off, and a child's beloved plush toy was rendered missing only to be found in plain sight the next day. The guest also spoke to the beds being made before the attendants had been in to do the daily housekeeping services.

When SyFy's *Ghost Hunters* checked out the resort with their plethora of equipment, their EVP machine showed most activity around Carolyn's room.

But there is a regal aura to Carolyn who mourns her husbands with refined grace. After all, Room 314 is referred to as the Princess Room.

Omni Mount Washington Resort

Address: 310 Mt. Washington Hotel Rd., Bretton Woods, NH 03375

Website: www.omnihotels.com/hotels/bretton-woods-mount-washington

THE SOUTHERN MANSION

Cape May, New Jersey

The Southern Mansion bed-and-breakfast is one of the largest and most opulent mansions in New Jersey and the only New Jersey B and B with a Four Diamond Award. Contracted by Philadelphia industrialist George Allen in 1863, his seaside palace was a favorite destination of Allen and his descendants for over eighty-three years. After the last of Allen's direct heirs passed, the property and furniture sold for pittance and the mansion fell in disarray. Fortunately, inspired by an old lithograph of the mansion in its glory days, it was restored in the mid-1990s. Once known by the Southern gentry as "Up North Down South," the current mansion retains the antebellum architecture and the flavor of a Southern city estate in the mid-nineteenth century.

Guests will find that the area surrounding the mansion is as elegant as the mansion itself. The nearby Willow Creek Winery gives tours and samples, and guests can stroll the elaborate fifty-acre garden and vineyards and even visit the roaming game cocks. Cape May is known as the "Restaurant Capital of New Jersey" and guests will find seafood, Creole, and French cuisine on nearby Jackson Street.

For those who prefer water sports, head to Cape May in the summer for kayaking, sailing, enjoying stretches of long beaches, fishing, and charter boats. The Southern Mansion staff can ensure surfers are given a surfing lesson with a world champion!

The Southern Mansion itself is as much a museum as it is a comfortable getaway. Hand-painted shower tiles, claw-foot tubs, and an evening turndown service are all included in the experience. Each room features authentic antique furniture, and the staff are happy to provide beach towels and chairs for excursions waterside. There is a gourmet breakfast menu made to order as well as a daily buffet of scones, muffins, pastries, coffee, tea, and juice.

 THE GHOST of the Southern Mansion is Ester Mercur, George Allen's niece. Fortunately she is a friendly ghost who seems to wander the mansion and its grounds to enjoy the restored furniture and rooms she was accustomed to when she was living.

But given the oldest seashore resort in the state has hosted visitors for over 250 years, it stands to reason a few others have lingered. Many believe the ghosts were always there, though some staff and attendants are certain that they were rustled to the afterlife by the renovations. Room 14 seems to be particularly active with paranormal activity. Guests attest to being awoken at midnight by an invisible conversation between a ghost couple at the edge of the bed. The chef who has worked at the Mansion for over twenty-one years maintains he is not scared, though—not even when he saw a figure in military clothes wandering in the kitchen only to vanish altogether in the hallway. According to him, they are friendly spirits and occupy the space. There are some things, apparently, you cannot explain. That doesn't mean they are necessarily malicious though.

When SyFy Channel's *Ghost Hunters* visited Cape May they found there was much more to explore in terms of paranormal activity and guests should seek ghosts in the hotel, yes, but also beyond. Jackson Street is said to have many haunted areas, Congress Hall is heavy on haunted activity and the Cape May Lighthouse is not just scenic for its spectacular views—but for its spectacular specters. Finally, guests should visit Cabana's Beach Bar where they will relax while an Irishwoman cast out for having a child of out of wedlock roams silently and mournfully while they sip their drinks.

The Southern Mansion

Address: 720 Washington St., Cape May, NJ 88204

Website: www.southernmansion.com

LA POSADA DE SANTA FE

Santa Fe, New Mexico

The stylish La Posada de Santa Fe features attractive adobe-style cottages contain the guest bedrooms, while the main facilities are contained within an old Victorian inn. The whole property is situated among six beautifully landscaped acres of gardens, right in the heart of downtown Santa Fe.

Wood-beam ceilings, hand-carved southwestern furniture, and paintings by local artists all testify to the hotel's authenticity. There are 119 traditional guest rooms and suites in all, and regular visitors suggest it is worth asking for one of the ninety rooms with their own Indian kiva-style (or beehive-shaped) fireplaces.

Because of the two contrasting styles of building, each room is different and could be described as reflecting some stage of Santa Fe's history. Vigas, bancos, and other elements of traditional adobe construction rub shoulders with the refinements of the resort. Special attention was given to ensure that all 157 restored casita-style rooms and suites honor the resort's heritage as an art colony.

The grounds are lush with centuries-old pine trees, quaking aspen, and blossoming flowers—a wonderful setting for relaxation. Santa Fe lies close to the foothills at the southern tip of the Rocky Mountains, and the hotel's central situation puts the plaza—starting point for viewing the historic city center—and museums within easy walking distance. With dining recently featured at the James Beard House and a patio serving tapas around open fire pits, it is no wonder that La Posada is one of the stops on the Santa Fe margarita trail. Guests will also enjoy the curated on-site art gallery as well as the ministrations of the on-site spa.

 THE GHOST at La Posada de Santa Fe is Julia Staab—and while she may be a ghost, she is also one of Santa Fe's best-known and best-loved characters. Julia was the wife of Abraham Staab, who in 1882 built the house, which is now part of La Posada. Abraham Staab, a German immigrant, made his fortune as a major supply contractor for U.S. Army posts in the Southwest during the Civil War and became a highly respected citizen of Santa Fe. He returned to Germany to find a bride and came back married to the former Julia Schuster.

The couple moved into their beautiful brick house (it has since been stuccoed to look like adobe) in 1882, and Julia became one of the town's leading socialites, furnishing her house in smart eastern style and holding weekly afternoon teas "at home" in the yellow silk drawing room.

Behind the glitter, Julia led a troubled life. A conscientious mother, she was heartbroken when her baby son died after an illness lasting several weeks. Her hair turned white overnight. Determined to raise a large family, she had seven children in all. But there were medical complications, and eventually Julia died on May 14, 1896, at the age of fifty-two. Glowing obituary notices were mixed with a whiff of scandal, for Julia had not been seen at all during the final years of her life. It was said she'd gone crazy and had to be locked up. Certainly, she has shown no inclination to leave her former home.

People who have seen her have always described her as wearing "a dark flowing gown and a hood."

She is usually seen at the top of the grand staircase in the central building in the main complex of the inn. But she has also been spotted in the Nason Room, a small alcove off the main dining hall. These later appearances are interesting because the Nason Room is a relatively recent addition. In Julia's time this was a garden.

A former employee at La Posada, Alan Day, reported in 1979 that he was cleaning in the Nason Room late one night when the hotel was deserted and looked up to see a woman standing by the fireplace. She was wearing a long dark gown and was translucent, he said, "but I could see her dark eyes looking at me." With remarkable composure, Day returned to his cleaning. When he looked up again, the figure had vanished.

Often Julia is just a "presence," noticed by employees and accompanied by a sudden and unexplained draft or seen and always "beautifully dressed."

She certainly doesn't seem vindictive: perhaps because from a salon to a social club to a restaurant and even a renowned margarita, the workers and guests at La Posada honor her memory.

La Posada de Santa Fe

Address: 330 E. Palace Ave., Santa Fe, NM 87501
Website: www.laposadadesantafe.com

ST. JAMES HOTEL

Cimarron, New Mexico

The St. James Hotel, now a national historic property, began as a saloon built in 1873 by the Frenchman Henri Lambert, who had been personal chef to Presidents Lincoln and Grant. At that time, Cimarron (it means "wild" or "untamed" in Spanish) was a stop on the Santa Fe Trail, a really wild hangout for traders, mountain men, and desperadoes.

To begin with, the new hotel was a place of violence. Twenty-six men were killed within the two-foot-thick adobe walls. The notorious gunfighter Clay Allison is said to have danced on the bar, now part of an elegant dining room, which still has bullet holes in the pressed tin ceiling.

But today the hotel is a place of quiet elegance, fine food and drink, expert and friendly service, and unsurpassed hospitality. Guests can dine at either Lambert's or TJ's bar.

The St. James Hotel offers thirteen restored bedrooms, all beautifully decorated with antiques. Most have private facilities, but guests will find options for singles, doubles, and family rooms on the website. These rooms are complemented by a modern twelve-bedroom annex, where all rooms have private bathrooms.

Situated in the scenic foothills of the majestic Sangre de Cristo Mountains, the St. James Hotel is surrounded by excellent hunting and fishing areas, and is only minutes away from the Angel Fire and Red River ski resorts. Visitors can also enjoy the outdoor splendor of Valle Vidal Park and the Palisades in nearby Cimarron Canyon.

THE GHOSTS at the St. James Hotel are a trio of characters straight out of a Western movie, which is hardly surprising when you consider this property was once a rough, tough, Wild West saloon. There is Mary Lambert, the wife of the hotel's builder, Henri Lambert, who still inhabits her old room on the second floor; gambler James Wright, who came to a sticky end right after winning a big poker hand; and a sort of poltergeist known simply as "the Imp."

James Wright is by far the most fascinating of the three. His presence was first noticed in Room 18 while the hotel was being refurbished in 1985. The reports were sufficiently convincing for the room to be shut and locked. It has been locked ever since.

Jacque Littlejohn, a psychic from Albuquerque, identified the mysterious presence as Wright. His winning poker hand earned him a huge prize, variously reported as an entire herd of cattle or even the hotel itself. But before he could collect his winnings, Wright was murdered. And, Littlejohn says, Wright's spirit is still waiting in the hotel to collect his winnings.

Fanciful stuff. Except that when the owners came to inspect the old hotel registers, they discovered a gambler called James Wright had indeed checked into the hotel just before the killing. His room number? Yes, you've guessed it—eighteen.

Meanwhile, Mary Lambert is still taking a friendly interest in the people who stay in the building her husband created. Guests frequently smell her perfume, and women brushing their hair sometimes get a helping hand from Mary, whom they feel touching their heads. Hotel historian David Kenneke has reported that both sensations are stronger if Mary likes the guests.

The aptly named Imp seems to confine himself to the kitchens and the bar, annoying staff by moving implements and bottles and, sometimes, causing these items to float through the air.

The hotel was restored from old photographs to the way it looked in the 1870s. Gunfights and gambling were common events in the saloon and the customers included Jesse James, Clay Allison, Wyatt Earp, Bob Ford, Buffalo Bill Cody, Bat Masterson, and Pancho Griego. This was not a bar to brawl in. Twenty-six recorded shootings took place in the saloon, with Clay Allison responsible for eleven of them. When a new ceiling was installed in 1902, more than four hundred bullet holes were found in the old one. No wonder the place is believed to be haunted. But one-time owner Greg Champion pointed out the ghosts for which the St. James is now famous for do not haunt the hotel.

They merely live there.

St. James Hotel

Address: 617 S. Collison Ave., Cimarron, NM 87714

Website: www.exstjames.com

THE ALGONQUIN HOTEL
Manhattan, New York

For visitors wanting a luxurious visual memory of their time in NYC, this Forty-Fourth Street landmark is a quintessential Manhattan experience. Designed by architect Goldwin Starrett, the twelve stories in Renaissance limestone and red brick towered over the city when the hotel (then private residences) opened in November 1902.

Today, the boutique hotel features 181 guest rooms complete with complimentary Wi-Fi and well-lit writing desks in case guests are as moved by the muse as some of its famous writers in residence.

The hotel's interior history is as glamorous as its outer facade: from the cat always kept in residence to the once-dry hotel fashioning a $10,000 martini (a glass of the guest's martini of choice with a diamond in lieu of ice). But the Algonquin is best known for its Round Table: populated by a different sort of knight than those found with King Arthur. Journalists, actors, authors, poets, and philosophers have long flocked to the Algonquin and their conversations still echo throughout. From Dorothy Parker to Harpo Marx, the engaging conversation in the main dining room are preserved in the hotel's dedication to its rich history. The Oak Room is also renowned having hosted its fair share of premier cabaret guests from Harry Connick Jr. to Diana Krall.

THE GHOSTS of the Algonquin Hotel are many of its famous patrons who checked in—but never checked out. Such an illustrious guest roster especially appealed to one Gawker journalist who brought a checklist of the many famous guests and a Ouija board to ask and quickly assess who was still around. She certainly got more yeses than nos or maybes.

From disembodied footsteps in empty hallways to ghostly apparitions hovering in the lobby and the dining room, it seems that many of the hotel's famous patrons still haunt in search of their muse.

The Oyster Travel website refers to the Algonquin Hotel as "the best haunted hotel" and I can assume they are not speaking to the elegance and ritzy nature of the dining room or art deco. Yet, given its history, maybe this speaks to the caliber of the spirits found still chatting and roaming therein.

The Algonquin
Address: 59 W. 44th St., New York, NY 10036
Website: www.algonquinhotel.com

BELHURST CASTLE

Geneva, New York

Belhurst Castle is a turreted, red-stone building constructed in the latter half of the 1880s. The name Belhurst means "beautiful forest." Sitting atop a cliff among sweeping lawns and tree-shaded vistas, it overlooks Seneca Lake and combines the romance of the past with the comforts of the present in an elegant yet relaxed atmosphere.

Belhurst Castle is centrally located in the middle of the Finger Lakes region, about one hour's drive from Rochester, Syracuse, and Corning. Sonnenberg Gardens, Watkins Glen, the Finger Lakes wineries, and Hobart and William Smith Colleges are all within easy reach.

Guests of the Belhurst will enjoy the bounty of the Belhurst winery complete with tasting options and the opportunity to bring a few bottles home.

The Belhurst also specializes in craft beer to be sampled during your stay or to be purchased for later. For dining, guests can choose the in-castle sophistication of Edgar's Restaurant and experience the grandeur of the castle's past or, the comfy and relaxing Stonecutter's Tavern, which highlights handcrafted cocktails and traditional pub fare.

Within the chambers of the castle eleven guest rooms are available while guests can also stay in one of the exterior cottages: Dwyer Lane, Carriage Castle House, or Ice House. The Vinifera Inn on the castle grounds offers twenty modern guest rooms: each featuring Jacuzzies and an in-room fireplace. Finally, the White Springs Manor reflects a 1900s Georgian-revival farm once home to the largest herd of

Guernsey cattle. Whatever your fancy, the Belhurst caters to every last experience of Gilded Age castle life.

 THE GHOST at Belhurst Castle is that of a beautiful Italian opera singer, who fled from Spain to America with her lover in the late eighteenth century and now seems reluctant to leave the gardens of what became her home.

The couple had good reason to flee Spain. Two men had fallen in love with the opera singer at the same time: a handsome young man and an older, married Spanish don. Within a few weeks, the handsome young man was dead from multiple stab wounds. The don was the chief murder suspect. Pursued by the authorities, as well as the don's humiliated wife and family, the opera singer and her murder-suspect lover escaped to America. There they joined up with a band of trappers and eventually arrived in the Finger Lakes region, where they set up home in a house that once stood on the site now occupied by Belhurst Castle.

The couple believed they would never be found there. But just in case, they had an emergency escape route, a secret tunnel running from the cellar of their house down to Seneca Lake.

For two years, the couple lived happily in their lakeside hideaway. Then one day their pursuers caught up with them, bent upon revenge for the humiliations they had suffered. The couple raced for their secret tunnel. Just as they were within sight of safety, the tunnel collapsed, killing both the opera singer and her pursuers.

The disconsolate don escaped. Brokenhearted, he spent the rest of his life in a monastery, grieving for his lost love.

All this is a well-known story locally but is almost certainly based more on fantasy than fact. No one can even be sure that the runaway coupled existed. And yet . . .

The secret tunnel would have run under what is now the castle lawn. Stories persist that it is still there. And, over the years, dozens of guests at the inn have reported seeing a woman in white standing silently on the front lawn in the middle of the night. Could it be the opera singer revisiting the spot where she died?

Another phenomenon sometimes reported by guests is the sound of someone singing to a baby during the night, even when there is no young mother or child staying at the inn. How this links up with the story of the romantic runaways is not clear. But a property such as Belhurst Castle ought to be surrounded by legends like this, for they complement the atmosphere of romance and add a touch of mystery.

Belhurst Castle

Address: 4069 W. Lake Rd., Geneva, NY 14456

Website: www.belhurst.com

North Carolina

THE BILTMORE
GREENSBORO HOTEL

Greensboro, North Carolina

Guests can expect hospitality as old as this building when they stay at the Biltmore Greensboro where the owners boast that little things like a favorite room or a late checkout are always remembered. Moses and Ceasar Cone moved to the city in 1895 with the Cone Export and Commission company and soon became known as "denim pioneers." When the Cones sold the company, their building assumed numerous identities from an annex and post office to upper furnished private residences, an apartment building and now the hotel. The owners of the now-hotel in the 1930s brought in famed interior designer Otto Zenke, who lent his design an English hunting-lodge style of walnut paneling that is still reflected in the lobby and rooms. Grand canvas portraits and furniture pieces from the time of the inaugural owners provide each of the twenty-six rooms a quiet ambience.

THE GHOSTS of the Biltmore Greensboro are Philip, a former accountant for the Cone brothers, and Lydia, a woman who once went by the name of Wendy. Philip was found dead in a nearby alley with a piece of piano wire and the speculation of suicide surrounding his death. Once his office, Room 332 is where Philip is most often found apparently enjoying haunting female guests in particular. Guests have reported noisy footsteps and shuffled paper—an eager accountant still keeping the books in order.

During a period when the building was used as a residence solely for female tenants, Lydia (then known as Wendy) was thrown over the balcony to her death. Her room, 223, is now painted pink and there is a lingering belief that by wearing pink you honor her spirit and stay on her good side. Guests record a pink purse situated under the dresser and a pink lipstick in the closet to appease her restless spirit. But nothing seems to calm Lydia on restless nights. She likes to run the water and rearrange the toiletries on the bathroom counter. Her lingering perfume becomes a strong floral reminder as she comes and goes but never truly leaves.

In a news segment, the general manager attested to the activity inside, "There have been many people with good intentions and bad intentions that have walked these halls and its possible some of their energy has been trapped inside."

Yet the hotel website posts a warning to guests: "The hotel does not advertise or make claim to any kind of ghost or paranormal activity." The warning goes on to say that ghosts are a matter of opinion and belief and thus perform their bookings and guest reservations without guarantee of a certain room. The ownership states their opinion that the paranormal rumors are little more than passed-down stories. The brave guest will have to decide if the ghostly encounters at the Greensboro are told for mere entertainment value, or if there is something far more sinister at play.

The Biltmore Greensboro Hotel

Address: 111 W. Washington St., Greensboro, NC 27401
Website: www.thebiltmoregreensboro.com

OMNI GROVE PARK INN

Asheville, North Carolina

The rough-hewn stone facade of this iconic mountain lodge is most distinctive when set against the sunset over Sunset Mountain. The Blue Ridge Mountains are renowned as some of the most compelling and photographable in the world. It was fortunate, then, that "the Father of Modern Asheville," Edwin Wiley Grove, began accumulating land bit by bit and taking possession of the neighboring farmland until he built—slowly and surely—to the top of Sunset Mountain.

The Omni Grove Park Inn has a rich and varied history long beyond Grove's lifetime. For instance, during WWII it served as an internment center for Axis powers. Beyond the many presidents who have enjoyed time here, guests such as George Gershwin, Harry Houdini and F. Scott Fitzgerald have found reprieve and solace in the Blue Ridge Mountains.

Guests who visit the inn today can expect eighteen-hole golf, an on-premises spa, and a yearly National Gingerbread House Competition worthy of the most popular Hallmark Christmas movie.

The on-site spa includes steam rooms, hot tubs and restorative hot tubs and has been noted as one of the world's best. As for dining, there are several options to meet every taste. Elaine's Dueling Piano Café promises relaxation and excitement combined while Edison Craft Ales and Kitchen will provide guests the opportunity to sample fare indigenous to the Appalachian region of the Blue Ridge Mountains. Cocktail terraces at the higher altitudes of the hotel give guests a wonderful view of the surrounding hills and mountains.

 THE GHOST of Grove Park Inn is the "Pink Lady": the spirit of a woman who fell to her death from a balcony on the fifth floor in the 1920s. She usually appears in a pink mist or even wearing a pink ball gown. She is known to be a nice and approachable spirit who bears guests no ill will. The Pink Lady keeps vigil by the bedsides of ill guests—with a particular affinity for children. Reports document a doctor staying at the inn who wrote a note to the proprietors thanking the "lady in the pink ballgown." Room 545 is supposedly where she fell to her death and, subsequently, where she prefers to spend her time.

Though you may see the Pink Lady, the gray granite walls of the historic hotel may usher safe passage for many other ghouls and specters. Clearly with magnanimous history comes the high possibility of spirits.

Omni Grove Park Inn

Address: 290 Macon Ave., Asheville, NC 28804
Website: www.omnihotels.com/hotels/asheville-grove-park

ROUGH RIDERS HOTEL
Medora, North Dakota

When the Rough Riders Hotel was built on the edge of the Badlands in 1884 it was known as the Metropolitan. Founder George Fitzgerald fashioned it as an exact replica of his Merritt House Hotel in Glendive in what was then known as the Montana Territory.

The name was changed in 1905 to honor Theodore Roosevelt and his cavalry of cowboy soldiers whom he led in the Spanish-American War. There is Roosevelt history aplenty not only in the Rough Riders Hotel but in Medora altogether as the town of a little more than one hundred does what they can to draw tourists to revisit the history of the prolific hunter-turned-historian-turned-president.

Roosevelt once gave a speech on the hotel's then-balcony and guest room shower tiles to this day feature the three brands he used on his cattle during his time in the Dakota Badlands.

There are no fewer than seventy-six historical plaques (many dedicated to Roosevelt) throughout the hotel as well as the largest private library (over one thousand volumes) of books available for guest viewing.

Guests will be able to choose from four types of available rooms included those with queen and double beds, double queens and double king beds, and a historic rough rider named suite. Guests will also have access (season permitting) to the outdoor pools at the nearby Badlands Hotel. There is a fitness center available and free Wi-Fi and some rooms have minifridges. Guests will find nearby attractions including the Cowboy Hall of Fame close by.

Theodore's Dining Room is another homage to the president with Old West touches and raved-about dishes including steak and bison osso buco.

THE GHOST of the Rough Riders Hotel is surprisingly not Theodore Roosevelt (who as we learn in another segment of this book is busy at the Menger Bar and not a two-timing ghost) but a nameless youngster. No one is quite sure from whence he came or why he so enjoys the Rough Riders Hotel. Perhaps it is because of its spacious and rustic surroundings with long corridors through which he can laugh and play. He does, however, have a mischievous side and a penchant for toilet pranks— flushing them when no one is around, watching and waiting for the reaction of unsuspecting people to acknowledge his joke.

It was before the hotel's most recent renovation, about a decade ago, that workers encountered the unexpected—a constant guest who wouldn't leave despite the numerous changes and updates.

And visiting guests should be warned that the constant guest still hasn't vacated the premises.

Rough Riders Hotel

Address: 301 3rd Ave., Medora, ND 58645

Website: www.medora.com/stay/hotel/rough-riders-hotel/

Ohio

PUNDERSON
MANOR LODGE

Newbury, Ohio

The Punderson Manor Lodge is an English Tudor-style estate that now functions as a hotel and conference center on Punderson Lake. The property was first owned by Lemuel Punderson for whom the lake and surrounding area are now named. In the early 1920s a Detroit businessman, Karl Long, began to transform the manor house to what guests will enjoy today. Guests will find thirty-one rooms in the main house either in the Old Tower section of the hotel or the newly refurbished quarters. There are also twenty-six two-bedroom cabins that are pet friendly and ideal for extended stays. Old or new, each room is outfitted with antique reproductions matching the Tudor themes of the lodge. With a cocktail lounge and full-service dining room, guests have every convenience at the ready. The lodge encourages guests to take advantage of golf specials and even participate in overnight Murder Mystery events.

In the summer months, the proximity to Punderson Lake make

it perfect for swimming, hiking nearby trails and kayaking or take advantage of the basketball and tennis courts. In the winter, snow-mobilers, cross-country skiers, and snowshoers find plenty to explore.

 THE GHOST of Punderson Lodge is, for many, Karl Young who lost everything, including grand plans to expand his mansion and estate, and is believed by some to have killed himself in the attic of the mansion of which he had such high hopes. Others believe the apparition they encounter to be that of Lemuel Punderson who, in an equally strange legend, floated out to the middle of Punderson Lake in a bathtub before pulling the plug and drowning (contrary accounts cite he died of malaria). There's also the tragic story of an 1885 hotel fire that destroyed the Wales Hotel, once directly across from the Punderson, killing several children whose voices can still be heard having drifted over the lake and into the rooms of unsuspected lodgers.

In 1979, park employees encountered the gruesome sight of a man hanging by the neck from a rope tied to the rafters of the lodge with the haunting site swinging for three hours before drifting into the mist. TVs turn on and off, taps run when no one turns them on and even in unoccupied rooms children's laughter floats. Cold breezes from cold windows and footsteps, of course, cement the Punderson as one of Ohio's most haunted places.

The most haunted room, 231, is dubbed "the Blue Room" and is now known as the Windsor Suite. Here, a young woman taking a shower pulled back the curtain to find the wastebasket had been moved and was now blocking the doorway, keeping her in. One flustered gentleman had just checked in before frantically approaching the front desk begging to check out. Hearsay says his wife had sat on the bed and wasn't able to get up because of all the ghosts holding her down.

Whatever the spirits are up to at Punderson Lodge, one thing is clear, they don't want you to leave.

Punderson Manor Lodge

Website: 11755 Kinsman Rd., Newbury, OH 44065

Address: www.pundersonmanor.com

THE SKIRVIN HILTON

Oklahoma City, Oklahoma

A towering art deco in the center of the Bricktown Historical District, the Skirvin Hilton Hotel places guests within easy access of Chickasaw Bricktown Ballpark, the Civic Center Music Hall, and Film Row. A member of the Historic Hotels of America and the National Registry, the hotel is named for founder Bill Skirvin and opened in 1911. Today, the hotel retains its magnificent structure and exterior while providing guests with deluxe comfort. Often a host for visiting sports teams, guests may just catch a glimpse of their favorite basketball or baseball player.

Guests of the 225 rooms and suites have access to an indoor swimming pool and fitness center, high-speed internet, bathrobes, black-out curtains, and in-room coffee. The Red Piano Lounge is the perfect place to relax with live music and seasonal events such as a yearly Thanksgiving Feast and a Christmas High Tea are easily booked on their website. For dining, the Park Avenue Grill boasts live music and varied breakfast, lunch, and dinner menus. Though the hotel closed in disrepair in 1988, it reopened in 2007 after extensive renovations that preserved historically accurate windows and the original exterior finishes but also provided more accommodations, like elevators and accessible suites for inclusivity. But despite its modern touches, the draping chandeliers and wrought-iron railings add a distinctively historical elegance to magnificent downtown structure.

 THE GHOST of the Skirvin is rumored to be a former maid named "Effie," whose affair with founder Bill Skirvin resulted in a pregnancy. Determined to hide Effie and save his reputation, Skirvin supposedly locked her in a tenth-floor room even after she had her baby. Depressed and entrapped, Effie is believed to have jumped, with her baby, from the tenth-floor window to her demise. Apparently Skirvin kept this sordid affair and its tragic aftermath so well hidden, as there was no newspaper record of it. But the lack of real evidence has puzzled guests and historians for years. Historically the tenth floor is where gambling and all manner of vices took place in the Skirvin's earlier heydays.

What seems to be real is the many visiting NBA basketballs teams who have encountered Effie, or at least some form of haunted presence. The hauntings are so real to the players many have made international news. In 2010, for example, the visiting New York Knicks publicly blamed a loss to the Oklahoma City Thunder on the hauntings. The Chicago Bulls were also unhappy with the strange sounds and independently slamming doors interrupting their sleep. When the Miami Heat were in town for the 2012 NBA Finals, they, too, reported that the ghosts threw off their game. So is the legend real or not? According to sources, Brooklyn Nets player Kyrie Irving is determined to pursue the truth with the development of a feature film investigating the hotel's paranormal activities.

But it is not only the famous ball players who have had run-ins with Effie. Cleaning staff members report moving something to one place only to find it in the exact opposite spot from where they moved it. Whether Effie is real or not, the paranormal activity in the Skirvin Hilton Hotel is far from a figment of someone's imagination.

The Skirvin Hilton
Address: 1 Park Ave., Oklahoma City, OK 73102
Website: www.skirvinhilton.com

HECETA LIGHTHOUSE BED AND BREAKFAST

Yachats, Oregon

The history of the lighthouse and its innkeeper's residence are as interesting as the area itself. The Heceta Lighthouse is the most powerful marine light on the beautiful Oregon coast and has been since it was first lit in 1894. Renowned as one of the most regal lighthouses in America and featured on PBS's *Great Lighthouses*, the lighthouse was named for Spanish explorer Don Bruno de Heceta who set sail from Mexico in 1775 and identified the headland on which the lighthouse is nestled. For many years keepers and their families lived at the "light station" which had its own post office and one-room schoolhouse. The last keeper at Heceta turned off the manned light in summer 1963 and it has been automated ever since.

Fortunately for tourists to Oregon's famous coast, it was converted into a bed-and-breakfast with dollops of old-world charm. Guests of the B and B can expect a leisurely seven-course breakfast with a rotating seasonal menu prepared by owners Carol and Mike who are also certified executive chefs. The six guest rooms feature spectacular ocean views, historic touches, and claw-foot tubs. Guests can relax and explore in the rest of the house and sit in the intimate ocean view parlor or recline on the grand Victorian wraparound porch where sea lions, whales and eagles are frequently spotted. A daily wine and cheese allow guests to sample some of the state's best wineries and creameries. Nighttime light tours will help guests familiarize themselves with the unique history of the lighthouse and get a glimpse of the rotating lamp they may see from their bedroom window.

THE GHOST of the Heceta Lighthouse Bed and Breakfast was identified by a Ouija board as having the name "Rue." The wife of a one-time lighthouse keeper, her young daughter perished by falling over the cliff, and Rue still keeps watch in the lighthouse keeper's quarters, maybe scanning the sea and its magnificent rocky cliffs in hopes of a sighting.

Caretakers, historians, students, and guests have long reported hauntings—even before the current owners Mike and Carol Korgan refurbished the station into the charming B and B it is today. Several recorded ghostly interactions include the finding of a headstone in the vegetation around the property, an 1890s silk stocking placed where a tin of rat poison was set and windows open and closing of their own accord. One worker cleaning the attic windows noticed a woman's reflection beside his own in the pane and turned around to encounter a white-haired woman behind him. When attic glass was shattered on another occasion, caretakers found carefully swept piles of glass before they had the opportunity to attend to it. Fire alarms ring with no battery and overnight guests become familiar with the sweeping sounds of furniture being moved and a pale figure in Victorian garb pacing the empty and locked attic. The inn's six rooms may house fifteen prospective guests each night but no more . . . perhaps because the attic is already occupied.

Heceta Lighthouse Bed and Breakfast

Address: 92072 Hwy. 101 S., Yachats, OR 97498

Website: www.hecetalighthouse.com

TILLIE PIERCE HOUSE INN
Gettysburg, Pennsylvania

Current innkeepers Gail and Bob hope you share the privileged excitement they have of being an integral part of American history. After all, their inn not only reflects the simple pleasures of the Victorian era in beautiful Pennsylvania but reflects the travesty and world-changing events of the Civil War. Guests of the Tillie Pierce House Inn can expect to learn much about daily life during the Civil War and the years leading up to the momentous Gettysburg battle. There are romantic packages available to book as well as Battlefield Experience packages to delight the history-lover. Located directly in the historic town square, guests are in walking distance of many of Gettysburg's attractions. Grab and go breakfast items as well as one hot entrée are offered each morning and all rooms have private bathrooms. While there is Wi-Fi throughout the house, there are a few rooms without televisions though a common room with a TV is on the floor. There are six rooms available including one named for the eponymous Tillie herself.

THE GHOST of the Tillie Pierce house is Matilda "Tillie" Pierce who like many Gettysburg residents witnessed some of the bloodiest days in American history. Tillie was only fifteen years old when the Battle of Gettysburg was fought. From her window she witnessed the Confederate Army march into town. Later, Tillie's recollections published as *At Gettysburg, Or What a Girl Saw and Heard of the Battle* was a popular resource in understanding and reliving the fateful events. Tillie's bravery at rushing to aid the wounded soldiers, even as a teenager, was a harrowing experience. She held hands, helped amputate appendages, and sewed up wounds with rudimentary experience. The ghosts of the soldiers that Tillie tended to apparently still remain at her childhood home. Guests have recorded seeing soldiers in full regalia keeping watch.

It may be these tragedies that keep her spirit alive and roaming. While guests consider Tillie's room to have a presence, the room now known as the Lydia Leicester Suite has its own fair share of history. On the night of July 2, 1863, this room housed Major General George Mead who used it as headquarters while he met with officers. Many believe this room is haunted by the presence of the men who met there. Footsteps of soldiers or even a man sitting at the edge of the bed are common occurrences to those seeking the paranormal. There is even rumor of a poltergeist cat roaming the halls.

Amateur investigators and ghost hunters by the dozen have taken to YouTube to share videos of their experiences and findings. Many assuring that none of the spirits trapped in Tillie's house are malevolent. It stands to reason—like the town of Gettysburg itself—they are merely trying to make sense of the tragedy that occurred well over a century ago while finding new ways to honor its legacy.

Tillie Pierce House Inn

Address: 301 Baltimore St., Gettysburg, PA 17325

Website: www.tilliepierce.com

GRADUATE PROVIDENCE

Providence, Rhode Island

Built in 1922, the Graduate Providence features 294 recently refurbished rooms still bearing the elegance of the hotel's previous identity as the Biltmore. Guest reviews remark on the great downtown views and the size of the rooms for their reasonable price. Guests are assured that the hotel is pet friendly and are given access to a complimentary fitness center and bike rentals. The Graduate Providence is in easy walking distance of many sightseeing activities. For those wanting a slightly different excursion, the Top Golf Swing Suite is available for rentals and catering from the hotel's sports themed bar.

Reiner's offers a sporty flare with a wide arrange of pub food, hand crafted cocktails, craft beer and an international wine selection. Guests on the go can stop at the Poindexter: the inn's in-house café for coffee and treats.

Close to numerous of the state's colleges and academic haunts, guests will find easy walking access to the most beautiful campuses in America. Visitors can book a historical tour of the city, or one of the many daytime and (haunted) nighttime boat tours.

Providence by the Book: A Literary Walking Tour peels back the curtain on the city's rich literary history and features the stories of famous resident authors H. P. Lovecraft and poet Sarah Helen Whitman—one-time fiancée to Edgar Allen Poe. The tour stops at the Providence Athenaeum where guests are treated to a view of its beautiful old library.

THE GHOST of the Graduate Providence is a once successful businessman who checked into the hotel on the fateful eve of October 27, 1929. The next morning, upon learning of the market crash, he plummeted from his fourteenth-floor window to his death. Now guests swear that walking by windows on the floor, his spirit reenacts the death over and over again, like Sisyphus doomed to repeat his task and never quite making it to restful peace.

But there is far more macabre at play given the hotel's original financier. A proud Satanist, Johan Leisse Weisskopf helped spread his religion as far as he could in the city. In the 1920s, around his time, the hotel's concealed and underground bar acted as a speakeasy relieving the restriction of Prohibition. During this era, the hotel witnessed the conversations of many corrupt politicians and cops who were implicated in numerous murders. Guests report that the spirit of the Speakeasy is alive with specters and strange noises. Glasses clink in a phantom toast and the raucous paranormal energy recalls century-old parties long into the night. In fact, the energies in the Graduate Providence are believed to have provided the inspiration for spooky stories like the A&E show *The Bates Motel*.

Graduate Providence

Address: 11 Dorrance St., Providence, RI 02903

Website: www.graduatehotels.com

South Carolina

20 SOUTH BATTERY

Charleston, South Carolina

This neoclassical boutique hotel offers sweeping views of downtown Charleston and is situated near the Cooper River and directly across from White Point Gardens in Charleston's historic district. The period detailed furniture such as four-poster beds and giant armoires. Featured art and artifacts such as tapestries and chandeliers make the hotel seem as much a museum as a comfortable and relaxing reprieve from Charleston sightseeing.

20 South Battery offers a nightly wine and cheese reception for guests as well as a European-style breakfast. Guests can take advantage of seasonal packages and discounts that include food, shopping, and trips to nearby plantations.

THE GHOSTS of 20 South Battery appear to be a lady in white, a Civil War solider and a small child. The hauntings date back to just after the Civil War and have continued through the inn's many redevelopments including, the most recent, as the Battery Carriage Inn. From strange sounds emitting from turned off cellphones to glowing shapes, the ghosts are a lively sort. As for sightings, guests have experienced a growl when they have attempted to make physical contact with the spirits. The most haunted rooms are Room 3, Room 8, and Room 10—each with a special brand of spirit manifestation. Room 10's ghost, for example, is known as the Gentleman Ghost. A grayish shadow that moves elegantly and enjoys startling reclining guests on the bed. In Room 8, guests usually sense a small child though one skeptic who meant to prove the rumors wrong found himself in the company of a headless torso and became a believer. In Room 3, guests describe glowing shapes or merely the chill and presence of someone being there. One married couple recorded their experience on Ghost City Tours. The husband's cell phone, which was turned off, woke the couple up in the middle of the night. It wasn't even ringing! Rather, it was omitting a noise they never heard before.

Said to be the most haunted inn of the South, guests are encouraged to end a day of sightseeing with many of the haunted and ghost tours in the area before retreating to their rooms to (try) to get a good night's sleep.

20 South Battery

Address: 20 S. Battery, Charleston, SC 29401

Website: www.20southbattery.com

BULLOCK HOTEL

Deadwood, South Dakota

A genuine piece of the old Wild West in historic Deadwood, the Bullock Hotel must have come as a bit of a relief to the townspeople when Sheriff Seth Bullock built it over the remains of his burned-down hardware store in 1895. Until then, gentlemen could find a bed only in one of the local bordellos or flophouses—ladies had nowhere to stay at all.

The original Bullock Hotel was considered one of the finest hostelries in the West. And it still is. Meticulously restored to its former grandeur, it offers new Victorian furnishings, big beds, hospitality bars, and, in some suites, Jacuzzi tubs.

But some things never change. Gaming still goes on around the clock at the twenty-four-hour casino with flashy slot machines and complimentary wine and beer for players.

Bully's Restaurant and Lounge serves thick cuts of steak and fresh seafood beside a crackling fire, and the meals are complemented by fine wines and imported beers. Buffalo Bodega Steakhouse offers karaoke and a large menu as well as theme nights.

The hotel is situated in the heart of Deadwood, which has been re-created as an old lead mining town. There are dozens of historic gaming halls all along Main Street and countless museums and other attractions. Mount Rushmore, Wind Cave, Badlands National Park, Devils Tower, and Spearfish Canyon (of Dances with Wolves fame) are all only a short drive away.

 THE GHOST at the Bullock Hotel is "Old Seth" Bullock, the first sheriff of Deadwood and a character straight out of the Wild West. His friends included Wild Bill Hickok and Calamity Jane, although he didn't think much of either of them.

Bullock's life story reads like a film plot. Born in Ontario, Canada, in 1849 to a Scottish mother, he quickly clashed with his army officer father's strict code of discipline and left home to "go West, young man." A politician at twenty, and a founder of Yellowstone National Park at twenty-three, he was a sheriff in Montana by the time he was twenty-four. When he joined the Gold Rush to South Dakota in 1876, he was a natural choice as one of the leaders of the lawless community that sprang up around Deadwood Gulch. He was appointed town sheriff in 1876 after the death of Bill Hickok, masterminded the rebuilding of what is now the Bullock Hotel, became a rancher, fought as a captain in the Spanish-American War, and befriended a man named Teddy Roosevelt. When Roosevelt became president, he appointed Bullock a US Marshal. Upon Roosevelt's death in January 1919, Bullock erected a monument to him in the famous Black Hills of Dakota on the crest of the newly renamed Mount Roosevelt. Bullock died later the same year.

That might have been the end of the story but for two very strange postscripts. First, in 1991, the owners of the Bullock Hotel got a letter from British psychic medium Sandy Bullock, saying that a spirit named Seth Bullock was trying to make contact and was giving the name of Deadwood in America. Could he be a relative, he wondered? And secondly, during reconstruction work on the Bullock Hotel in 1993, resident proprietor Mary Schmit, her employees, and several workmen all experienced a series of strange phenomena.

Schmit and her aunt, who lived with her at the hotel during reconstruction work at the time, often heard their names being called when there was no one there. A massive new bar with a twelve-foot plate-glass mirror, in the lobby awaiting installation, fell over with a crash that shook the building—but without breaking the mirror. At the back of the lower floor, which seems to be the most haunted part of the hotel, employees heard footsteps when there was no one around. Two reported seeing a tall shadowy figure in cowboy dress. Schmit's sister, Susan, was alone in the building when she heard the pots and pans being clattered in the kitchen, and promptly locked herself in the cellar for the night. There, according to Mary Schmit, Susan "smoked an entire pack of cigarettes—and she doesn't even smoke."

The British Bullock, Sandy, said he was getting his messages through a Sioux named Singing Water. He might indeed be related to Old Seth. He has nothing to gain financially from either his "family" connection or his revelations, and, oddest of all, he has answered ambiguous test questions, submitted by American experts, quite correctly. But for a man who has never been to America, he does seem to have something of a fixation with the characters more easily found in Western films than western folklore.

And for guests, the hotel prides itself on its feature on *Unsolved Mysteries* and its easily booked ghost tours.

Bullock Hotel

Address: 633 Main St., Deadwood, SD 57732

Website: www.historicbullock.com

NEWBURY HOUSE

Rugby, Tennessee

Well over one hundred years ago, the settlers who founded Rugby enjoyed comfortable lodging at this charming, mansard-roof boardinghouse. And guests can still stay there today, for Historic Rugby, the company that now runs the old town, has restored Newbury House and opened it to overnight guests.

Now the house boasts six individual rooms in the main building as well as three self-catering cottages on the grounds. Guests have access to a suite with kitchen and parlor on the main floor, a fireplace with gas logs as well as a coffee station complete with a goodies jar. While there is currently no on-property dining, there is an on-site commissary with limited weekday hours and the nearby R. M. Brooks where guests can grab lunch.

Historic Rugby is a touch of Victorian England in the Tennessee Cumberlands. More than one hundred years ago, its British founder described it as "a lovely corner of God's earth." Now the National Trust calls it one of the "most authentically preserved historic villages in America." Even more colorfully, and fitting for a settlement intended to be a utopia, one writer described it recently as "utopia in the wilderness."

Listed in the National Register of Historic Places since 1972, Rugby stands in a rugged river gorge setting where more than twenty of its decorative, gabled buildings remain. Christ Church Episcopal, the Thomas Hughes Library with its collection of seven thousand Victorian volumes, the Kingstone Lisle cottage, and the Schoolhouse Visitor Center are all within walking distance.

 THE GHOST at Newbury House is an Englishman named Mr. Oldfield, who in the 1880s was sent out from London to report on the progress of what was then a fledgling British colony.

"He liked the place so well, he sent to England for his son and wife to join him. But he died of heart failure at Newbury the night before his son arrived," says Barbara Stagg, former executive director of Historic Rugby, Inc.

Rugby was founded in 1880 by Thomas Hughes, the English social reformer and author of Tom Brown's School Days. Hughes envisioned a utopian community atop the beautiful Cumberland Plateau of East Tennessee. He planned an attractive little town, full of lawns, ornamental gardens, and gravel walkways, overlooking the gorge of the Clear Fork. The town, which Hughes named after the school in his book, had to be hewn out of the wilderness. By 1884, about 450 latter-day British colonists had moved in. Some local Americans, mostly skilled craftsmen and farming families were invited to join the community, which was run on Christian Socialist lines. There was a single interdenominational church. For all Hughes's forward-looking philosophy, however, the town, which he called "the new Jerusalem," quickly became an upper-class, English-style settlement with a very Victorian atmosphere. Everything stopped for afternoon tea, and everyone dressed for dinner.

But drought, fires, an outbreak of typhoid, and the place's sheer inaccessibility took their toll. Many of the settlers soon moved on. Hughes died in 1896, having lost $35,000 of his own money on the project. It was not until the 1960s that attempts began to preserve what was left of the town.

Since then, both restorers and the new residents are aware that the town's former residents still seem to be in occupation. The town is one of the most haunted in America and proud of it. "At the Halloween Ghostly Gathering each October, we share our 'spirited' history with visitors, calling up the spirits of our dear departed 'Rugbeians,'" Barbara Stagg explained.

That should be a spine-chilling occasion at Newbury House, where several guests have reported waking in the night to find the ghostly figure of a man bending over the bed—particularly in rooms two and four.

It might be Mr. Oldfield, looking for his beloved son. But there is another possible explanation, because when Rugby was built it had a hostelry called the Tabard Inn, named for the inn in Chaucer's Canterbury Tales. Utopia or no, the manager of the Tabard Inn murdered his wife in Room 13 by cutting her throat, then poisoned and shot himself.

A few years later, the Tabard Inn was destroyed in a fire. But the colonists were able to save some of the contents of the inn, including much of the furniture from the fateful Room 13. Some of the furniture found a new home in Newbury House, where it remains to this day. And who knows what spirits might have moved with it?

Newbury House

Address: Rugby, TN 37733

Website: www.historicrugby.org

Texas

MENGER HOTEL

San Antonio, Texas

———

A stone's throw from the Alamo and within walking distance of the winding River Walk—the artery that winds through the heart of San Antonio—the Menger Hotel's classical two-storied structure and Spanish courtyard garden provide the perfect escape. While the structure has undergone renovations in the past century and a half, architect John M. Fries's inspired vision still rests at the core of a site so steeped in heritage, a visit is to pull back the curtain of history.

As well as its connection to one of the most famous battle sites in US history, its rich tapestry will appeal to Civil War enthusiasts and visitors who hanker after tales of the Old West. Once a boarding place for Confederate soldiers during the War between the States and commandeered many of the hotel's guest rooms, the years after the war found it a key stop for cattle drovers on the Chisholm Trail and a meeting place for cattle barons expanding their influence across the West during the Reconstruction period.

Some of its famous residents include Theodore Roosevelt. A drink at the famous Menger Bar will find patrons at the site where Roosevelt recruited the men of the first volunteer US Calvary, more famously known as "the Rough Riders." When the men weren't training to fight in the Spanish-American War, the Menger Bar provided a needed reprieve.

The nearby old missions of San Antonio as well as the Spanish architecture provide a flavor perfectly suited to nighttime rambles under the tolling bells of the San Fernando Cathedral. Not far from the Market Square, the Spanish Governor's Palace and its unique adobe architecture, are a glimpse into the eighteenth century. The stucco one-story structure, pergola, and Spanish colonial–styled rooms are apparently as haunted as the Menger itself.

The Menger Hotel offers thirty-six elegant guest rooms and suites, an option of dining at Menger Bar or the Colonial Room, and in-hotel shopping at Davy Crockett's Cabin (home to unique books, gifts, and toys) and J. Adelman Antiques, Art, and Estate jewelry.

THE GHOSTS of the Menger Hotel are as varied as the history itself. In such a large hotel adjacent the Alamo, it is no wonder restless spirits have found the modern-day comforts perfectly suited to their afterlife appearances. One ghost is said to be Jim Draper, who was killed in the Menger Bar by H. H. Childers (the latter who represented Woodrow Wilson's presidential run in 1912). Guests can still see a bullet hole in the wooded barroom. Others have seen Richard King of King Ranch who kept a personal suite in the hotel for his trips to town and died at the hotel. Maybe he has unfinished business that keeps him roaming, again, in the direction of the bar. Then, there is the belief that old bully Teddy Roosevelt returned. Teddy sits nursing a drink in his old uniform and guests can see and sense him as clear as day. Finally, there is the apparition of the

Lady in White who offers a more refined chilling experience than the rough-and-tumble male spirits trapped in the hotel. Guests wonder how she could have taken residence there, for a woman of her time period could not have afforded a room. Colored clothes were a luxury afforded the rich and she is always draped in ivory.

Guests who buy ghost tour tickets from Sisters Grimm, located within the hotel, are offered a discount for one of their many walking or bus tour adventures.

Menger Hotel

Address: 204 Alamo Plaza, San Antonio, TX 78205

Website: www.mengerhotel.com

Utah

BIGELOW HOTEL AND RESIDENCES

Ogden, Utah

With almost three hundred rooms, suites, and private residences, the Italian Renaissance–revival hotel has held its spot as one of the grandest hotels in Utah since its opening in 1927. Guests can recline by the fireplace in the lobby as well as enjoy a complimentary hot buffet breakfast. The hotel's restaurants include a coffee shop, Irish pub, and upscale American restaurant. In-room coffee, free Wi-Fi, express checkouts, and laundry facilities make it a perfect destination for both business and leisure travelers. The mountain views and proximity to many of Ogden's must-see buildings, old and new, make it a prime location. Inside, the hotel's unique interior design acts as a bit of a world tour. From the Arabic-style coffee lounge to a Florentine Palace-inspired ballroom there is even a touch of old Spain in one of the business rooms.

The Bigelow Hotel and Residences is within close distance of the Treehouse Children's Museum, the Utah State Railroad Museum, and the Hill Air Force Museum—all perfect for family outings.

THE GHOST of the Bigelow Hotel and Residences spends most of her time in Room 1102 where she drowned on her honeymoon. Now water in the tub runs on its own, often turned by a phantom hand. According to hearsay, not long after her death, her son came to collect her personal effects. Overcome by the tragedy of his mother's demise, he took his own life. Now visitors report seeing them together in the afterlife: keeping each other company in the grand hotel that oversaw their untimely demises.

But there are other spirits trapped in the grand walls of the Bigelow: moving in and around and hijacking elevators that start and stop and journey to odd destinations without a pattern. The hotel's Prohibition-era history might also contribute to the phantoms in residence. In the 1920s, the hotel had a tunnel created with the intent of smuggling alcohol but ironically giving access to criminals for whom the party has yet to stop.

Bigelow Hotel and Residences

Address: 2510 Washington Blvd., Ogden, UT 84401
Website: www.bigelow-hotel-ascend-ogden.h-rez.com

GREEN MOUNTAIN INN

Stowe, Vermont

Built as a private residence in 1833, the Green Mountain Inn became a gracious hotel in the mid-1800s. Tastefully restored for its 150th anniversary, the inn today offers a warm blend of modern comforts and authentic country charm.

Each of the guest rooms and suites has its own special character. Many have queen-size canopy beds, fireplaces, and Jacuzzis. Stenciling, draperies of early American design, and country quilts all help to create an atmosphere of old-fashioned ease. For those guests wanting to stay in Stowe longer either for skiing or leisure, apartments and town houses are available.

Dining is in one of the inn's two acclaimed restaurants. The famous Whip Bar and Grill, named for its collection of buggy whips, is casual. Guests can also enjoy the dinner fare at 18 Main, which also provides to-go orders.

Guests enjoy complimentary use of the inn's fully equipped health club and heated outdoor swimming pool as well as a massage center. The Stowe Recreation Path offers strolling, jogging, and biking among beautiful mountain vistas. In the heart of Stowe Village, the inn is surrounded by restaurants, boutiques, and antique shops.

In winter, Stowe is justifiably known as "the ski capital of the East," with forty-five superb alpine trails on Mount Mansfield, Vermont's highest peak, and approximately 93 miles of groomed trails for cross-country skiing enthusiasts. No wonder the Von Trapp family, of *The Sound of Music* fame, settled here. It must have felt just like home.

THE GHOST at Green Mountain Inn is Boots Berry, a tap dancer and local hero who can still be heard dancing on the third floor of the hotel during severe winter storms. Boots Berry's connection with the Green Mountain Inn in general, and with Room 302 in particular, was extraordinary. The son of the inn's horseman and a chambermaid, he was born in Room 302 in 1840. At that time the third floor of the hotel was the servants' quarters, and the boy grew up in and around the building. When he was in his twenties, he succeeded to his father's job.

Boots was a respected horseman. One of his duties was to provide fresh horses for the daily stagecoach. So he was on the spot in the main street of Stowe one summer's morning when the team bolted. Boots bravely stopped the runaway stage, saved the lives of the passengers, and was awarded a hero's medal. News of his exploit spread and, in the words of a local newspaper report, "Boots' popularity was such that there wasn't a place in the county where he could pay for his own drinks."

That was to be his downfall. Boots turned to a life of wine, women, and song, neglected his duties at the inn, and eventually had to be dismissed. He then wandered the country, picking up his nickname when he was jailed in New Orleans and learned to tap dance from a fellow prisoner.

Eventually, at the beginning of 1902, Boots drifted back to Stowe, shabby and poverty-stricken. At about the same time, a dreadful storm hit the town and a little girl somehow got stranded in the snow on the roof of the inn. But Boots, remembering his own childhood days, knew of a secret route to the spot where the child was, climbed up to her, and lowered her safely to the ground.

Just as the girl reached safety, Boots slipped and fell to his death from the icy roof. His life had come full circle, for the roof he was standing on when he fell was the roof of Room 302.

If the sound of tap dancing on stormy days is anything to go by, he is still around. One member of staff even claims to have met him in the corridor. Former marketing director Darcy Walsh believes that Boots is a spirit to be proud of, and adds, "Most of us here believe there really is a ghost at the inn."

Green Mountain Inn

Address: 18 Main St., Stowe, VT 05672

Website: www.greenmountaininn.com

THE MARTHA WASHINGTON INN

Abingdon, Virginia

Set deep in the quiet Virginia countryside, in the charming town of Abingdon some three hundred miles from Richmond, is a beautiful mansion built in 1830 for General Francis Preston. It is now the wonderfully atmospheric Martha Washington Inn.

Having survived the ravages of the Civil War and almost one hundred years as a girls' school, the former Preston house could almost do duty as a living museum. Many of its original features are preserved, enhanced by period furnishings and antiques, and a degree of comfort and service that recalls the gentler lifestyle of our forefathers.

At "Martha's," as this historic home is affectionately known, the sixty-three guest rooms offer the highest degree of modern comfort. The silverware at dinner in the main restaurant, Sister's, is of the period, too,

There is a wonderfully ornate art deco dining table sixteen feet long that had been "lost" in the rambling cellars below the house. It is almost impossible to avoid superlatives—the garden lawns are immaculate, with camellias and magnolias.

Guests can enjoy a wind-down complimentary glass of port every evening in the main parlor as well as access to the "round table" in the inn's extraordinary library where a private collection of American literature is ready to peruse.

Guests who choose to dine at the on-site restaurant, Sister's will receive a credit on multi-night booked stays and a continental breakfast awaits each morning. The inn also features a swimming pool and hot tub, cycling, golf, and a 24-7 state-of-the-art fitness center.

Abingdon is a delightfully Victorian town, its shops featuring fashions, antiques, and fine arts and crafts. The famous Barter Theater has a full seasonal program. There are beautiful national parks nearby around Mount Rogers, and the Appalachian Trail passes close. The Virginia Creeper Trail originates in Abingdon and follows a historic and scenic route to the foot of White Mountain.

 THE GHOST at the Martha Washington Inn is Beth, a student at Martha Washington College during the Civil War. The inn had become a girls' school just before the Civil War broke out. As hostilities became increasingly violent, the house was turned into a hospital, with college staff and students doing their best to nurse the wounded of both sides.

One day, a Yankee officer, Captain John Stoves, was among the seriously wounded brought to the school. Confined to a room on the third floor and to the care of Beth, a girl with staunch Confederate sympathies, Stoves was too severely wounded to survive. Despite Beth's tender care and her prolonged attempts to keep him alive, Stoves's strength waned.

As the end drew near, Stoves called for Beth, an accomplished violinist who often cheered the wounded with lilting songs and bright tunes.

"Play me something, Beth. I'm going," Stoves whispered. And, for the last time, Beth played the soft, beguiling Southern melody that had comforted him so often.

After Stoves died, the weeping Beth, weakened by watching at his bedside through so many long nights, took to her bed. A few days later she, too, died—some say of the typhoid so prevalent at the time; others say of a broken heart. The Yankee soldier and his Rebel nurse now lie side by side in Abingdon's Green Springs Cemetery.

Whatever the cause of her death, Beth's playing of soft Southern songs on her violin can still be heard echoing faintly through the rooms on the third floor of the Martha Washington Inn, especially on nights when the moon floats full over the mountains.

Beth's spirit is not lonely at the inn, for there are two other ghosts known to frequent it.

One is the ghost of a young Confederate soldier who was in love with an Abingdon girl during the troubled time when the town was caught between Confederate forces to the west and Union troops to the east.

Entrusted with a dispatch for General Lee describing the Union forces' position and strength, the young soldier broke his journey at Martha Washington College to bid his sweetheart goodbye. Creeping up the stairs, he was surprised by a reconnoitering party of Yankees, who fired on him.

The rash youngster fell at his sweetheart's feet in a pool of blood. And his blood stained the floorboards so deeply that the marks are still there. Every effort to remove them has succeeded only temporarily. Today they are covered with carpet, in what is now known as the Governor's Suite.

Love of a different kind has given the Martha Washington Inn its third ghost.

On a moonless night in December 1864, Abingdon fell victim to its first invasion by Union troops. The Yankees were few in number and were routed by Confederate forces. But one Union soldier escaped on horseback along the alley east of the school before being felled by a chance shot. The wounded soldier was carried into the college, where he died just as the clocks of the town struck midnight.

The Yankee's horse would not leave its master. The animal followed him on to the school's grounds and restlessly paced the lawns waiting for him to come and ride. At midnight, as his master died, the horse silently left the college gardens and was never seen again.

Well, almost never. For sometimes, on a dark and moonless night, a ghostly riderless horse is seen waiting on the south lawn.

The Martha Washington Inn
Address: 150 W. Main St., Abingdon, VA 24210
Website: www.themartha.com

THE HISTORIC CAVALIER HOTEL AND BEACH CLUB
Virginia Beach, Virginia

Not many hotels and resorts claim they put a city on the map, but the Historic Cavalier Hotel and Beach Club in Virginia Beach boasts it did just that. It has more than loaned to the allure of the state with its prime beach location. Construction began on the hotel in 1926 and in a Jeffersonian-styled architecture with details that recall the former president's famous estate Monticello. Upon its opening, the Cavalier was added as a non-stop train destination from Chicago giving city folks the opportunity to get away in luxury. Famous guests include numerous presidents and some of the world's most famous performers including Fatty Arbuckle, Bing Crosby, Judy Garland and Doris Day.

During WWII, the Cavalier fell on hard times with the nation and its young men called to duty overseas. Then, the Cavalier was giving a different role to play: a radar training station. But there were too many men and not enough room so cramped soldiers allegedly even slept in the stables that once housed the grand horses used for elegant beach riding excursions.

Today, guests have a choice of eighty-five rooms and suites with a beach club, swimming pool and club, and beachfront cabanas at their fingertips. Resort-wide charging at the restaurants and various amenities ensure guests can hit the beach without constantly checking for their wallet. A complimentary beach shuttle leaves the hotel frequently for the resort at Atlantic Avenue.

In the tradition of its lush history, the Cavalier offers numerous dining experiences: the Four Diamond Becca Restaurant and Garden, for one, and the Hunt Room, which features a contemporary interpretation of classic tavern fare. There are also several beachside bars and restaurants for frozen drinks and seafood.

 THE GHOST of the Historic Cavalier Hotel and Beach Club is Adolph Coors of Coors Beer fame. In 1929, Coors's body was discovered on the grounds of the Cavalier days after he checked into his sixth-floor guest suite.

The sixth floor remains the most haunted according to guests and staff alike. Eerily, even when the hotel has been closed in winter for renovations or when no guests are staying in the rooms on the floor, persistent phone calls plague the front desk. These aren't just any phone calls. The receiver hosts muffled jazz music from Gershwin and his contemporaries, some of Coors's favorite ditties of yesteryear. Sometimes windows open and close without a reason and sounds shuffle from dark corner.

The Historic Cavalier Hotel and Beach Club promises a luxurious and relaxing stay—that is if you stay well clear of the sixth floor.

The Historic Cavalier Hotel and Beach Club
Address: 4200 Atlantic Ave., Virginia Beach, VA 23451
Website: cavalierresortvb.com/cavalier-hotel

HOTEL SORRENTO

Seattle, Washington

Inspired by architect Harlan Thomas's passion for the Italian Renaissance architecture of Vittoria, Sorrento, Italy, and commissioned by clothing merchant Samuel Rosenburg, the Sorrento has lived many elegant lives since its opening in 1909. Settled in the historic First Hill neighborhood, its first guests were prospectors, entrepreneurs and curious tourists attending the Alaska-Yukon-Pacific Exhibition. Once home to the city's highest restaurant, with views of Mount Rainier and Lake Washington, the Sorrento proudly embraces its long history while continually upgrading to more comfortable modern amenities.

There are seventy-six rooms and suites in the Sorrento with all boasting touches reminiscent of the hotel's early days such as carved wood moldings, vintage furnishings and artwork and marble baths in near every room and designer suite.

Guests are offered three unique dining experiences on-site: the Fireside Room, with wood paneling and oversized leather sofas around a large eponymous fireplace; the bar, with its speakeasy atmosphere; and the Stella, with fine dining and a contemporary Italian twist.

Unlimited local and long-distance calling, a twenty-four-hour gym, Wi-Fi, and in-room coffee and tea are included in the hotel fee.

Hotel Sorrento is within close distance of the Seattle Mariners' stadium, the Great Wheel, the waterfront, and the Space Needle. St. James Cathedral, the historic Town Hall, Pike Place Market, and the Frye and Seattle art museums are also easily accessible. Called "the Italian Oasis" by locals, the Sorrento is the great start of a great getaway.

THE GHOST of the Sorrento is a figure unique to paranormal hunters because they cannot understand why she haunts it at all. Alice B. Toklas who prefers the fourth floor and Room 408 specifically. She is usually seen hovering under a black or white shroud. When she is near, lights flicker and glasses move unattended. Toklas, lifelong romantic partner of American writer Gertrude Stein and one of the few Americans part of the Paris avant-garde, died after a long illness in Paris, France. Her spirit, however, prefers the Sorrento. Filmgoers who enjoyed *Midnight in Paris* will meet a fiction Toklas; but paranormal hunters stalk the fourth floor in pursuit of the real thing. The Sorrento is proudly known as one of the most haunted places in Washington and have been known to host dinners in Toklas's honor complete, of course, with a following ghost tour.

Hotel Sorrento

Address: 900 Madison St., Seattle, WA 98104
Website: www.hotelsorrento.com

THE LOWE HOTEL

Point Pleasant, West Virginia

The Lowe Hotel's history is as fascinating and varied as the town of Point Pleasant itself. The town, named for the Battle of Point Pleasant, celebrates its heritage as the site of the first battle in Lord Dunmore's War. Nearly a century later, it was home to Point Pleasant's only direct involvement in the Civil War, and the courthouse (where munitions were stored) bore bullet holes in the wall as souvenirs before the building was revitalized in the 1950s.

The Lowe Hotel is a four-story building that has been in continuous operation since founded in 1901 by J. S. Spencer and named for him until just after the 1929 market crash when it was purchased by the Lowe family. Since the early 1990s, Ruth, Rush, and Marcia Finley have been at the helm determined to preserve the history of the hotel with personal touches that make guests feel at ease.

The ground-floor entrance has marble touches and lantern fixtures and is always seasonally decorated. A sofa once belonging to Lorne Greene (of TV's *Bonanza* fame) is one of the little pop culture or historical pieces of interest the Finleys enjoy collecting and sharing with guests.

There are suites that overlook the Ohio River, and all rooms boast antique furniture that recalls the earliest years of the hotel's operation. Once a society high point in town and the site of an elegant dance hall, there are nods to the lush 1920s decade the Lowe experienced before the crash and subsequent Great Depression.

While there is no on-site dining available, the front desk will be happy to offer you a cup of coffee as well as nearby restaurant recommendations. Guests will find themselves a stone's throw from the Point Pleasant Riverfront Park with its amphitheater, riverfront walking trail and historical murals that portray the battle for which the town was named.

Bu many people suggest waiting to visit Point Pleasant and the Lowe Hotel for spooky season—and no, not October, rather the annual Mothman Festival hosted annually in September.

 THE GHOSTS at the Point Pleasant Hotel are plenty. One YouTube ghost hunter documented their experience as a "real life *Shining*." But it is the Mothman legend that lures many.

The Mothman is said to be a seven-foot-tall man with red eyes and a giant wingspan. So popular is the legend, an iron statue was erected to the myth and Point Pleasant Mothman museum is open for curious and brave visitors. The Mothman legend is a result of a 1966 *Pleasant Register* article with an eerie headline, "Couple Sees Man-Sized Bird." According to history, a couple were out on a drive near Point Pleasant's TNT Area; thus named because of its proximity to the site for a WWII munitions plant. The flying man startled the entire town. In 1966 alone there were apparently over one hundred sightings of the Mothman but records show his observants were too scared to go on official record. While a professor at West Virginia University believes the Mothman could be a far more logical sighting of the American sand-hill crane—who has a large wingspan and can grow to the height of a smaller built man—the legends, lore, books, and movies are far more fun; hence *The Mothman Prophecy*. It is safe to say that the Mothman is embedded in West Virginia mythology and the Finleys will be happy to host you during Mothman season, tell you stories about the creature, and encourage you to seek him out on your own.

While the Mothman may hover near the Point Pleasant, the ghost residents at the Lowe Hotel are equally as active. On the mezzanine of the second floor you can anticipate the sight of a beautiful young woman in long nightgown dancing to a tune only she hears. The ghost is believed to be Juliette Smith, daughter of once-manager Homer Smith. Forbidden to marry the "unsuitable" local boy with whom she was madly in love, he married someone else while she remained a spinster. Perhaps she is waiting for his return, imagining herself in his arms on the hotel's once glamorous dance floor.

The third floor is the site of the most paranormal activity. Guests in a river-facing suite might encounter Captain Jim who stares out at the Ohio River for a boat that never comes into shore. Then, there is a squeaking tricycle and laughing boy who bounds up and down the long corridors.

Noted as one of the most haunted hotels in America, the Lowe Hotel's haunted meter is raised by its proximity to Mothman sightings. In short, a supernatural-seeker's dream. If you do record a video or picture of something paranormal or just plain weird, make sure you don't merely post it to social media, the Finleys would *love* to see it.

The Lowe Hotel

Address: 401 Main St., Point Pleasant, WV 25550
Website: www.thelowehotel.com

THE PFISTER HOTEL

Milwaukee, Wisconsin

When the doors of the Pfister Hotel first opened on May 1, 1893, it was acclaimed as the ultimate in elegance and style. That elegance is still represented by the hotel's showpiece: its fine collection of nineteenth-century Victorian works of art. More than eighty original oil and watercolor paintings are permanently on show in the grand hallways and public rooms. It probably is the largest collection of its kind in a hotel anywhere.

But the age of elegance is not only on show in the paintings; it also continues to be represented by the hotel itself. A recent restoration has combined this historic grandeur with modern amenities so that guests of long ago, such as President McKinley or even Buffalo Bill, would still recognize their surroundings even if baffled by the high-speed Wi-Fi for late-night Netflix streaming.

The 307 guest rooms and suites are all beautifully furnished and decorated, and the bathrooms are stunning. The Tower rooms offer a spectacular view of Milwaukee's celebrated lakefront, while the suites have a variety of amenities ranging from personal sitting rooms to Jacuzzis.

The lobby area in particular has been beautifully restored. It now contains the spacious lobby bar and lounge, overlooked by a dramatic ceiling mural of a clear sky-blue scene of heavenly cherubs, reminiscent of the lobby's original skylight.

For a midday meal or the regal Sunday champagne brunch, the Rouge is a Milwaukee tradition. Other restaurants are the Café at the Pfister, which is a European-style bistro, and the award-winning English Room—the hotel's dining showplace.

After one hundred years, the original "Grand Hotel of the West" is still just that.

 THE GHOST at the Pfister Hotel is an old man who most people think must be Charles Pfister, the founder of the hotel. Certainly, Pfister was very proud of the hotel, so it's only to be expected that he's still keeping an eye on things.

"No one seems to know who first spotted him, or when," former concierge Peter Mortenson once said. "But he has been reported on the landing of the Grand Staircase, surveying the lobby. Another time he was seen in the minstrel's gallery above the Imperial Ballroom, and yet another time up on the ninth floor in a storage area."

He has certainly left his mark with a special brand of haunting: that of touring MLB players. Many of the players are skeptics who believe his sneaky specter visits not only visiting teams but also the Brewers themselves.

CJ Wilson, formerly of the Angels, described the feeling of waking up after a restless night "uneasy, like we had bad Chinese food or something." While other players have merely accepted his presence as part of the adventure. Perhaps because Pfister doesn't cut such a sinister figure.

The sightings have always been late at night and have always been the same: a portly, elderly gentleman, well dressed and with a cheerful smile. And when the witnesses have been shown a picture of Charles Pfister—who completed the hotel building project started by his businessman father, Guido Pfister, in 1893, and named the property after him—they have always uttered cries of amazement and exclaimed, "That's him!"

At least, that's what people say. Finding someone who has actually seen the ghost, or identified him from his picture, is harder.

The Pfister Hotel

Address: 424 E. Wisconsin Ave., Milwaukee, WI 53202

Website: www.thepfisterhotel.com

HISTORIC PLAINS HOTEL

Cheyenne, Wyoming

For lovers of the Old West, the Historic Plains hotel is aptly named for the legacy of the American frontier so vividly captured in its surrounding terrain. Indeed, this 1911 hotel has hosted past presidents, celebrities, and cattle barons alike who have loaned to its reputation as a premier "jewel of the state." The grand hotel gobbles up nearly half a block with a facade that would have appeared opulently modern during the time of its construction. Designed by William Dubois, the most prolific architect in the state, the hotel boasts his knowledge and passion for current trends whose influences still appease guests today. From the dozens of windows like peering eyes over the street below to the foyer with its overlooking balconies a vantage of a deco-style chandelier and marble touches—a far cry from the primitive Old West adventures visitors will want to seek out. And yet the spirit of the West will not be hard to find for eager enthusiasts waiting to step back in time. From the Covered Wagon and Rodeo World of the Cheyenne Old West Museum or even those keen on seeking out the dinosaur fossils at the Wyoming State Museum, history is everywhere.

THE GHOST at the Wyoming Plains is Rosie, a thwarted woman in love. Legend finds Rosie at the Historic Plains on her honeymoon. One evening she goes in search of her husband who had yet to return from a promised few drinks in the lounge. Upon seeking him out, Rosie found him engaged in flirtation with a lady of the night. She observed them leaving only to follow close at hand to a room on the fourth floor. In a jealous rage, she shot them with her husband's gun before returning to the honeymoon suite and taking her own life.

Hotel guests report that laughing and crying can be heard—could it be the clash of the intimate conversation between Rosie's husband and his new *amour* as well as crying by the jilted Rosie? Both the bride and groom appear, her in a blue dress and him in a white shirt and black dress coat—the bride roaming the corridors, the groom either on the fourth floor or relegated to the basement. And the woman who came between them can also be found, wearing scarlet (naturally).

Historic Plains Hotel

Address: 1600 Central Ave., Cheyenne, WY 82001
Website: www.facebook.com/thehistoricplainshotel/

TRAVELER'S CHECKLIST

ALABAMA
- ☐ Malaga Inn, Mobile

ALASKA
- ☐ The Historic Anchorage Hotel, Anchorage

ARIZONA
- ☐ Copper Queen Hotel, Bisbee
- ☐ Hotel Vendome, Prescott

ARKANSAS
- ☐ Crescent Hotel and Spa, Eureka Springs

CALIFORNIA
- ☐ The Carter House, Eureka
- ☐ The Clift Royal Sonesta, San Francisco
- ☐ Hotel del Coronado, Coronado
- ☐ Abigail's Elegant Victorian Mansion, Eureka
- ☐ Gingerbread Mansion Inn, Ferndale
- ☐ Horton Grand Hotel, San Diego
- ☐ Mendocino Hotel and Garden Suites, Mendocino
- ☐ Noyo Harbor Inn, Fort Bragg
- ☐ Queen Mary, Long Beach
- ☐ The Hollywood Roosevelt Hotel, Hollywood
- ☐ Scotia Lodge, Scotia
- ☐ US Grant Hotel, San Diego

COLORADO
- ☐ The Stanley Hotel, Estes Park

CONNECTICUT
- ☐ Blackberry River Inn, Norfolk

DELAWARE
- ☐ The Addy Sea Historic Oceanfront Inn, Bethany Beach

DISTRICT OF COLUMBIA
- ☐ Omni Shoreham Hotel

FLORIDA

☐ Don CeSar Beach Resort, St. Petersburg Beach

☐ Herlong Mansion, Micanopy

GEORGIA

☐ Jekyll Island Club Resort, Jekyll Island

☐ The Marshall House, Savannah

HAWAII

☐ Ritz-Carlton Kapalua, Kapalua, Maui

IDAHO

☐ White Horse Saloon and Hotel, Spirit Lake

ILLINOIS

☐ The Congress Plaza Hotel, Chicago

INDIANA

☐ Story Inn, Nashville

IOWA

☐ Villisca Axe Murder House (Josiah B. and Sara Moore House), Villisca

KANSAS

☐ Hotel Josephine, Holton

KENTUCKY

☐ The Sire Hotel, Lexington

LOUISIANA

☐ T'Frere's House, Lafayette

☐ Lafitte Guest House, New Orleans

MAINE

☐ Castine Inn, Castine

☐ Kennebunk Inn, Kennebunk

☐ Rangeley Inn, Rangeley

MARYLAND

☐ The Blue Max Inn Bed and Breakfast, Chesapeake City

☐ The Castle, Mount Savage

☐ Kent Island Resort, Stevensville

MASSACHUSETTS

☐ Colonial Inn, Concord

☐ Omni Parker House, Boston

☐ Deerfield Inn, Deerfield

☐ Hawthorne Hotel, Salem

☐ Longfellow's Wayside Inn, Sudbury

☐ The Lizzie Borden House, Fall River

MICHIGAN
☐ The Terrace Inn, Petoskey

MINNESOTA
☐ The Palmer House, Sauk Centre

MISSISSIPPI
☐ The Duff Green Mansion, Vicksburg

MISSOURI
☐ The Lemp Mansion, St. Louis

MONTANA
☐ Chico Hot Springs Resort and Day Spa, Pray
☐ Garnet Ghost Town Cottages, Granite County
☐ Murray Hotel, Livingston

NEBRASKA
☐ Arrow Hotel, Broken Bow

NEVADA
☐ Gold Hill Hotel and Saloon, Virginia City

NEW HAMPSHIRE
☐ Omni Mount Washington Resort, Bretton Woods

NEW JERSEY
☐ The Southern Mansion, Cape May

NEW MEXICO
☐ La Posada de Santa Fe, Santa Fe
☐ St. James Hotel, Cimarron

NEW YORK
☐ The Algonquin Hotel, Manhattan
☐ Belhurst Castle, Geneva

NORTH CAROLINA
☐ The Biltmore Greensboro Hotel, Greensboro
☐ Omni Grove Park Inn, Asheville

NORTH DAKOTA
☐ Rough Riders Hotel, Medora

OHIO
☐ Punderson Manor Lodge, Newbury

OKLAHOMA
☐ The Skirvin Hilton, Oklahoma City

OREGON
☐ Heceta Lighthouse Bed and
Breakfast, Yachats

PENNSYLVANIA
☐ Tillie Pierce House Inn,
Gettysburg

RHODE ISLAND
☐ Graduate Providence,
Providence

SOUTH CAROLINA
☐ 20 South Battery, Charleston

SOUTH DAKOTA
☐ Bullock Hotel, Deadwood

TENNESSEE
☐ Newbury House, Rugby

TEXAS
☐ Menger Hotel, San Antonio

UTAH
☐ Bigelow Hotel and Residences,
Ogden

VERMONT
☐ Green Mountain Inn, Stowe

VIRGINIA
☐ The Martha Washington Inn,
Abingdon
☐ The Historic Cavalier Hotel and
Beach Club, Virginia Beach

WASHINGTON
☐ Hotel Sorrento, Seattle

WEST VIRGINIA
☐ The Lowe Hotel, Point Pleasant

WISCONSIN
☐ The Pfister Hotel, Milwaukee

WYOMING
☐ Historic Plains Hotel, Cheyenne